D1418136

CAN EUROPE

KEEP THE PEACE

This is a book of realities. Here laid out before your eyes is the true story of the explosive situation of present day Europe. There is no popularized crying of "Wolf, wolf!" Mr. Simonds paints no gaudy pictures; he does not tell you when the next war will come, what it will be like, or how to avoid it. But from twenty years of experience and observation, he gives you an accurate and detailed statement of what is going on in Europe and explains the problems about which we have all wanted to ask questions if only we could find a man who knew the answers.

America is filled with well-meaning earnest groups—largely women—who, knowing nothing much of European history and, filled with provincial and impractical notions of brotherly love, think all racial problems abroad are in some way evidence of "foreign inferiority" and can be settled by American sweetness and light. As Mr. Simonds points out:

"Woodrow Wilson was satisfied that he had only to appeal to the peoples, over the heads of their prime ministers, to obtain a peace of justice and understanding. But to all peoples beginning with the American, the Wilsonian appeals were without avail when they placed international dreams above national realities."

Mr. Simonds does not write in scare-heads. He makes no effort to rouse our fears of European conflict. But after reading this book, you will look at the map with a new and informed interest and ask yourself, "Can Europe keep the peace?"

CAN EUROPE
KEEP THE PEACE?

BY

Frank H. Simonds, Litt.D.

PUBLISHERS

NEW YORK *Harper & Brothers* LONDON

1931

CAN EUROPE KEEP THE PEACE?

Copyright, 1931, by Frank H. Simonds

Printed in the U. S. A.

SEVENTH PRINTING

A-G

TO MY SON

JAMES G. SIMONDS

MY COMPANION
ON MANY OLD BATTLEFIELDS
AND NEW FRONTIERS

Contents

Maps

Preface

FIVE years ago I wrote a book, which appeared in this country under the somewhat rash title, "How Europe Made Peace Without America." The French publishers more cautiously called it "L'Europe d'Après Guerre." That volume was written immediately after the entrance of the Germans into the League of Nations and, at that moment, I shared the common belief that Locarno had marked a decisive turn, alike in Franco-German relations and in the post-war history of Europe.

That hope proved, at least temporarily, unfounded. In the present volume, therefore, I have undertaken to examine in detail the issues, the policies and the states of mind of the European peoples, which collectively constitute the problem of peace, together with the experiments in international association, which have been made since the close of the World War.

The historian, presenting his book to the public, is able to fortify his statements by citation of his sources. The journalist's situation is quite otherwise. The report of the events, which he has witnessed, the description of the frontiers, that he has travelled, the record of national policies and opinions, which he has gathered, all stand undocumented. Their value depends, after all, uniquely upon his credibility as a witness and his ability as an observer.

The present volume represents twenty years of first hand observation of Europe in peace and war, beginning before the Second Balkan War of 1913, continuing through the World War and followed by many visits to the fronts of racial conflict since 1918. Its judgments of international meetings are based upon attendance at the Paris Peace Conference, the Washington Naval Conference and the still recent London Naval Conference, together with many of the Assemblies of the League of Nations.

In these years I visited French North Africa, Greece, Danzig, the Polish Corridor and Vilna; Galicia, the new Hungarian frontiers from Pressburg to Szeged; Trieste and the adjoining battlefront of Yugo-Slav and Italian; the new frontier of iron along the Maritime Alps and the old on either side of the Vosges. In London, Paris, Brussels, Rome, Warsaw, Prague, Vienna and Budapest, as well as at Geneva, I interviewed the public men engaged in making contemporary history, and I also met and exchanged views with the great figures of the European press.

In this time I have been the guest of people of

every degree of rank and absence of rank, enjoy-
ing the benefits of victory or enduring the miseries
of defeat in East Prussia, the Polish Corridor and
Hungaria Irredenta. I have visited regions in the
process of devastation during the World War and
in the similar process of devastation since the Peace
Conference. Everywhere people have, with utter
frankness, explained to me what life meant for
them in the conditions in which they lived.

Out of this long and varied experience I have
tried to construct a picture of contemporary Europe.
And I mention these personal details, simply because they are the sole *bona fides* which a journalist
may offer to counterbalance the footnotes of his
more—and perhaps less—fortunate friend, the historian.

F. H. S.

Blighty, Snowville, N. H.
October, 1931.

PART ONE

THE PARIS CONFERENCE

Chapter One

BALANCE OF POWER AND SELF-DE-TERMINATION

THE starting point of any examination of the problem of peace in contemporary Europe must logically be the Paris Conference of 1919. The reason is twofold. Like the Congress of Vienna, a century before, the Paris Conference gave Europe a political system destined to endure for many years. And, also, this historic gathering marked the first attempt of Democracy to reorganize the Old World in accordance with its own principles.

For the two centuries which separate the Thirty Years War from the close of the Napoleonic drama, international adjustments after general wars had been made by statesmen and diplomats in the service of dynasties and monarchies. Utrecht and Vienna were famous examples of this fact, and even as late as the Congress of Berlin, the pomp and circumstances of traditional Europe still survived and the machinery of old fashioned diplomacy was again employed. But at Paris, half a

3

century later, Democracy had come of age and peoples were masters of their foreign policies.

The measure of the change is supplied by the contrast between the Europe of 1815 and 1919. When the statesmen of Vienna had completed their settlement, Divine Right had been re-enthroned from one end of the Continent to the other. But, on the eve of the Paris Conference, republican care-takers were already installed not alone at Ver-sailles, but also in Sans-souci and the Hofburg, while Red Guards patrolled the corridors of the Winter Palace beside the Neva.

Disillusioned by the outcome of the Paris Con-ference, democracies have everywhere sought to repudiate responsibility for the failure by rejecting it upon the Europe which had vanished. But no effort could be more transparently dishonest. For it would be impossible to imagine more typical representatives of Democracy than the American college president, the French Jacobin and the Welsh psalm-singer, who were the "Big Three" of Paris. Nor is it less undeniable that the Congress and Parliaments which these statesmen represented at all times asserted and exercised the authority to accept or reject the decisions made in their name.

Since peoples were in control at Paris for the first time, and because, also, the issues which were there considered, have continued to dominate inter-

national relations, it is manifest that the proceedings of the Peace Conference supply an admirable
measuring rod. In fact, to understand clearly why
the Paris Conference failed, is to appreciate the
reasons for the persistence of anarchy in post-war
Europe.

The Settlement at Vienna had been frankly
based upon the doctrine of the balance of power.
Few political dogmas have, in their time, enjoyed
wider acceptance, or ended by falling into deeper
disfavor. For nearly two centuries and a half, it
constituted the single known prescription for
assuring the independence of the European Continent. By contrast, progressively in the years following the Congress of Vienna, it became a symbol of
tyranny and a basis for oppression.

Yet, at bottom, this doctrine of the balance of
power was no more than the embodiment of the
lessons taught by the experience of centuries, and
expressed the mature conviction of European
statesmanship that disproportionate power, lodged
in the hands of any monarch, was certain to prove
the prelude to an assault upon the territorial unity,
and even upon the independence of other states.
This doctrine had been painfully evolved in the
long struggles resulting from the various attempts
at Continental hegemony of the sovereigns of
Spain, Austria and France, and the recent experi-

ence of Europe, alike with Revolutionary and Imperial France, had given fresh weight to a principle, which had become traditional.

Despite all the odium, which has attached to this doctrine in later times, it was, nevertheless, based upon the conception of a Europe in which the collective right of all states to security, and therefore to peace, was set above the right of any king or emperor to expand, or even to consolidate his own territory, at the cost of others, and inevitably by war. And, if the doctrine could only rarely be invoked to prevent aggression, it was often and successfully employed to resist it.

At Vienna, therefore, while the conquerors of Napoleon were immediately concerned with the restoration of dynasties, which had been scattered by the Revolutionary and Napoleonic earthquakes, their main preoccupation was to create barriers, which would preclude a repetition of recent and familiar French aggressions. And this major purpose, which involved a fresh application of the doctrine of the balance of power, was their warrant for seating Austria in the Milanese and in Venice, for the transfer of Belgium to Holland, and for the establishment of Prussia on the Rhine, and even on the Sarre. And since proportionate additions in population and territory for Russia were not otherwise discoverable, it also explained the transfer of the bulk of the Polish people to the Czar.

To permit the application of the doctrine of the balance of power, peoples were thus distributed by the head like cattle, and provinces were parcelled like real estate. Only in the case of France were national and racial rights respected, and exception was made solely to insure the presence of a Bourbon on the French throne. But, contrary as the Settlement of Vienna was to all later conceptions of the rights of peoples, it must, nevertheless, be said for it, in justice, that not only did it achieve the end for which it was designed—since France was never able again to undertake the military conquest of the Continent—but also it gave Europe a full generation of relative tranquillity unbroken by any conflict between great powers.

It is, however, not less obvious that in re-ordering Europe in conformity which the doctrine of the balance of power, the statesmen of 1815 had founded their system upon a principle, which had already become obsolescent. For the great democratic explosion of the French Revolution had alike awakened the desire of peoples to rule within states, and of races to acquire liberty and unity. And the Settlement of Vienna did extreme violence to both of these democratic aspirations.

As a consequence, Napoleon was not yet in his

island tomb when the first shots fired in the Greek War of Independence ushered in a hundred years of national struggles. In 1830, the Belgians rose against their Dutch masters. Between 1830 and 1848, the Poles, the Magyars and the Italians took up arms against Russian and Austrian oppression. From 1859 to 1871, Europe was shaken by a series of national wars, which resulted in the unification of Italy and Germany. After 1871, the battle was transferred to the Balkans, and the Turkish War of 1912 ended by restricting Ottoman empire in Europe to the bridgehead of Constantinople.

From 1815 to 1914, therefore, all European wars, without significant exception, had found their cause or their occasion, in the resolution of peoples to attain liberty and unity. Even the World War, itself, was precipitated by the assassination of Serajevo, a crime wholly comparable to the Orsini affair, half a century before, which had been the prelude to Italian unification as the later murder was the preface to that of the Southern Slavs. Thus the whole history of a century was, in a sense, the record of the progressive liberation of the peoples of Europe, and when the Paris Conference assembled, the process was completed. From the English Channel to the Pripet Marshes, the majority of every race was now free, and the newly liberated peoples were clamoring to have their independence established by the law of Europe.

Manifestly, it would have been impossible in Paris in 1919 and in the light of the events of a full century, to have undertaken to apply the doctrine of the balance of power once more. Nor were the statesmen of the later congress under any temptation to follow the example of Vienna. On the contrary, from the very outset of the World War when Belgium was invaded, the Allied nations had been led step by step to endorse the rights and to champion the aspirations of the smaller peoples of the Continent under the domination of the Central Powers. When, too, Russia had fallen away to anarchy and separate peace, they were left free to extend similar endorsement to the claims of the Polish and Baltic peoples.

Expediency and self interest, quite as much as any concern for democratic principles, also dictated that the victorious nations at Paris should favor the smaller peoples, since the recognition of the claims of the Poles, the Czechs, the Rumanians and the Southern Slavs in every case involved a reduction in the area and population of the enemy states. And, in addition, before the Paris Conference assembled, the statesmen of the victorious nations had formally accepted the Fourteen Points of Woodrow Wilson.

This celebrated formula of the American President was, in fact, no more than an attempt to give concrete application to the lessons of the century which had been filled with the struggles of peoples to attain liberty and unity. It constituted a recognition of the rights of peoples to determine their own political association, and was thus as clearly the expression of democratic conception as balance of power had been of monarchial.

Contrary to the general American impression, too, this democratic conception, which at Paris was described as the right of self-determination, was not first formulated in the Fourteen Points. In reality, it was identical with that theory of nationality, which Napoleon III had evolved half a century before when he was endeavoring to establish a relationship between the French Revolution and the First Empire.

This principle of nationality had been applied in the case of Nice and Savoy in 1860, and the overwhelming majority for France in the plebiscite had silenced all criticism of the annexation of these territories. By contrast, condemnation of the course of Bismarck in 1871 was universally based upon the indisputable fact that the Treaty of Frankfort did utter violence to the will of the inhabitants of Alsace-Lorraine. And, in the mind of Woodrow Wilson, no idea was more firmly established than that of preventing the creation of any new Alsace-Lorraine.

In the century which separated the fall of Napoleon from the flight of William II, the principle of self-determination had, then, plainly superseded the doctrine of the balance of power as the basis for territorial adjustment in Europe. It had, in fact, become the accepted doctrine of a new democratic world. Moreover, in 1919, the material interests of the European victors, and the moral enthusiasm of the American President, combined to make it the basic principle of the Paris Settlement.

But the application of the principle involved consequences unforeseen by any of its advocates. And the first of these consequences arose from the ethnic circumstances of the European Continent, itself.

Chapter Two

ETHNIC EUROPE

IN THE Europe which existed before the French Revolution, the boundaries between races were without political significance. Provinces were transferred following the marriages and deaths of princes, or as a consequence of war, without regard for the desires of their inhabitants, who obeyed the new master with the same docility they had displayed toward the old. When, however, the right was vested in peoples to fix their own allegiance, since this decision was bound to be based upon race, ethnic limits assumed obvious importance.

Yet the smallest examination of the ethnic map of the European Continent discloses the fact that only in the west is the separation of races clear and unmistakable. There, Nature herself seems to have fixed the limits of peoples. Thus the British, Spanish, and Italian peoples are shut off from their neighbors by sea and mountain. And, in the same fashion, the French are protected by the west, the south, and the east by formidable natural bulwarks. Only between the Donon Peak in the Vosges, and the port of Dunkirk on the North Sea, is there a gap in the physical armor of France. And precisely on this front, Latin and Teuton have been in conflict from the campaigns of Julius Cæsar to those of Ferdinand Foch. Yet with the passing of the centuries, the struggle has narrowed to a battle for the possession of Alsace-Lorraine. Since, too, these "lost provinces" had been restored to France by the Armistice terms, their fate was not a cause for controversy in the Paris Conference.

But if the application of the principle of self-determination in the west of Europe presented no problem at Paris, in the central and eastern regions, the situation was utterly different. There, the great decisions had to be made, and there, too, in all the vast area bounded on the north by the Baltic and on the south by the Adriatic, Ægean and Black Seas, the ethnic map discloses an intermingling of races which, illustrated by colors, is kaleidoscopic in appearance.

In these Central and Eastern regions, too, no mountains, rivers or seas separate races as in the west. Pole and German are in shock on the great plain which stretches endlessly from the Urals to the battlefields of Flanders. On the Bohemian Plateau, the German-speaking population occupies the outer rim, the Slavic, the inner citadel about

Prague. In the vast Danubian Plain, Magyar, Slav and Rumanian have hated each other immemorially within the confines of the same villages, while in the Balkans, the chaos of quarrelling races has been proverbial for centuries.

Not only are there no natural lines of ethnic cleavage in all of these areas, but everywhere the racial fronts advance and retreat, bend in and bulge out in vast salients and deep pockets like the old battle front in France. And between the solid masses of races, there are no-man's lands, where tribes are inextricably mingled, and any boundary line, in dividing majorities, must create minorities.

Again, the ebb and flow incident to the rise and fall of states, the changes due to the migrations of peoples, the colonizations following conquest, have resulted in the creation of ethnic islands. Thus, the solid block of German population in East Prussia is separated from the Teutonic world by a Polish peninsula descending on the left bank of the Vistula to the sea. Similarly, half a million Magyars dwell in the great elbow of the Carpathians, isolated from the Hungarians of the plain by a wide band of Rumanian populations.

Cities, too, are frequently inhabited by peoples belonging to another race than that dwelling in the environs. Lemberg is a great Polish town in a Ukrainian countryside. Thorn and Bromberg were,

919, Teutonic islets in a Polish sea. Vilna, at the
e of the ethnic frontier between Lithuanian and
ite Russian, is Polish. On the very rim of the
st, looking down into the Italian city of Trieste,
villages are Slovenian. In Transylvania, while
manians and Magyars dispute the possession of
the province, the cities are Saxon.

Everywhere, too, racial differences are accentuated by religious. The Poles are Roman Catholics,
the Prussians Protestants. Invariably, also, religious
feuds are older than racial, and frequently more
acute. The Hungarians are both Protestant and
Roman Catholic, but their Rumanian and Serb
neighbors are Greek Catholic. Again, social and
political distinctions intensify racial rivalries. In all
this vast central region, the Germans, the Austrians
and the Magyars have long been ruling peoples
and, as such, have justified authority by a claim to
race superiority. But the Slavs and Latins have challenged the authority and resented the claim.

To apply the principle of self-determination to
all of this region stretching from the northern to
the southern seas, involved condemning minorities
to live under alien and oppressive rule, necessitated
placing Protestant populations under Roman Catholic rule, and Roman Catholics under Greek. It required the transference of power from the hands
of minorities accustomed to rule, to majorities with-

out experience. It meant taking control from the oppressor and bestowing it upon the oppressed, whose recent sufferings were bound to be a guide for future policy.

Application of the principle of self-determination to this hopeless jumble of races presented yet another problem, and that was to fix the limits within which the will of peoples was to be recognized. For in many areas, racial majorities could be made and unmade as frontiers were gerrymandered. Thus, on the lower Vistula, there would be a Polish Corridor extending from the Netze to the sea, or a German dam stretched from Pomerania to East Prussia, as the area was circumscribed or expanded. Upper Silesia would remain German, or pass in part to Poland, as the vote of the inhabitants was viewed as a whole or with regard for the result in the smaller divisions.

To all these complications history added yet another, for, turn and turn about, many races have ruled in the same area. There had been a Polish Corridor which antedated the voyage of Columbus and endured to the eve of the American Revolution. But the Teutonic Knights had ruled on either bank of the Vistula before Provence had passed to the French Crown. The Magyars defended the frontiers of the Crown of St. Stephen on the basis of a millenial title, but the Rumanians pressed their claims to portions of the same area as the descendants of the Roman colonists established by the Emperor Trajan. As for the Greeks, they founded their claim to Thrace upon Byzantine possession, and demanded Macedonia as the residuary legatees of that Philip, who was the father of Alexander the Great.

In the light of the ethnic conditions of the European Continent, it was therefore patent that the task of evolving any system of frontiers at the Paris Conference would not only be difficult in the extreme, but the most meticulous regard for the rights of all peoples, victorious and vanquished alike, could not remove the necessity to create minorities and to mutilate frontiers and, in fact, to make decisions which were bound to be unwelcome, and might prove intolerable.

Thus, the question of whether the settlement of Paris would prove a viable system of peace or a cause for fresh international conflict, was bound, in the end, to turn upon the accuracy of two necessary assumptions: First, that Democracy had been a moral as well as a political revolution, and that peoples, unlike their former rulers, were prepared to subordinate their national rights to a universal need for peace; second, that the recent war, which had covered the European Continent with ruins, and carried misery and death into every home, had brought peoples to accept the doctrine of peace at any price, measured in territorial and ethnic sacrifice.

It was, too, his faith, alike in the enlightened vision and the chastened spirit of peoples, which had led Woodrow Wilson to proclaim his Fourteen Points as a programme to make the World safe for Democracy. But was Democracy, in its present stage of evolution, safe for the world? The answer to this question was discoverable only by the examination of the evolution of democratic ideas, themselves.

Chapter Three

DEMOCRATIC NATIONALISM

THE desire of European races for unity, like that of the peoples of the Continent for political power within their own states, was born in the French Revolution. At the outset this great democratic upheaval was no more than a domestic revolt of the mass of the French people against the privileged classes gathered about the throne. As such it had derived patent inspiration from the American Revolution, and the principles of the Declaration of Independence had found authentic echo in the Proclamation of the Rights of Man.

When, however, the sovereigns of Europe undertook to restore the monarchy in France, and at the same time plotted a new Polish partition, this time on French soil, the whole French people rushed to the frontiers and Valmy became a national victory. The proud slogan "France—One and Indivisible" was too, the first clear expression of the spirit of democratic nationalism. But the French Revolution passed swiftly and significantly from defense to aggression, and in no long time capitulated to the imperialism of Napoleon. Nevertheless the spirit of Valmy did not perish; on the contrary, it found new lodgment in the hearts of the German people, and the armies of the First Empire encountered it fatally on the battlefield of Leipsic.

At the Congress of Vienna, the rights of man and of races were similarly denied, but with equal futility. For, in the generation between 1815 and 1848, not only did peoples seek domestic liberty, and races, ethnic unity, but they also marched together. Both were conscious that they faced a common enemy, since both were similarly struggling against the system established by the Congress of Vienna and sustained by the will and genius of Metternich. Thus, shots fired across the Parisian barricades in 1830, and again in 1848 were signals for racial insurrections to the Belgians, Poles, Magyars, and Italians. Even the German people hailed the triumph of the French mobs as their own.

After the failure and fiasco of 1848, however, a distinct change occurred, a change which was twofold, affecting peoples and their sovereigns alike. Metternich had disappeared and the great statesmen who followed him, Cavour in Italy, and Bismarck in Prussia, guided their royal masters along other pathways. Henceforth, the Savoy and Hohenzollern dynasties identified themselves with the national aspirations of their peoples. Victor Emmanuel thus became the soldier of the Risorgimento, William I, the successor of Barbarossa and Otto the Great, as a symbol of German unity.

Concomitantly, the people put the water of nationalism in the wine of their democracy. Sadowa and Sedan established a new entente between the German people and the Hohenzollerns. The manoeuvre henceforth associated with the name of Bismarck proved at once more skillful and more successful than Metternich's sterile policy of repression. Thanks to it, monarchy in Germany, gravely compromised in 1848, enjoyed a respite of half a century after 1870.

And, in fact, the attack of peoples upon their thrones in the name of Democracy, had terminated. After the collapse of the Third Empire, republican progress in Europe was arrested for half a century. Monarchs, secure in their new rôle, viewed with relative unconcern—save in Russia—the slow and minor progress of invasive parliamentarism. Peoples, intoxicated by the dream of national greatness, and satisfied by ever increasing material welfare, forgot the old democratic passions of 1792 and 1848.

All over Europe, this Bismarckian strategy was imitated. Francis Joseph, who began his long reign by ruthless persecution in Budapest, and relentless repression in Vienna, made terms alike with his Magyar and German subjects, and thus became the guarantor of the political supremacy of the ruling races on either bank of the Leitha. Even the Czars, while continuing to oppress their Polish subjects, adopted, not without a measure of success, the nationalistic gospel of Pan-Slavism.

A partnership between king and people was thus everywhere established, based upon common service in the cause of nationalism. And in Germany and Austria-Hungary, this partnership lasted right down to the closing weeks of 1918. Dissolution then, in the November "cascade of thrones," did not proceed from any spontaneous revival of the old democratic spirit, nor did it result from the fact that royal pretensions had suddenly become intolerable for peoples. It flowed uniquely from the fact that the profits of the association had visibly vanished. Long acclaimed the shining symbols and successful servants of satisfied nationalism, the Hapsburg and Hohenzóllern dynasties were ultimately suffered to depart into the wilderness as scapegoats for national disaster.

But what is most striking in itself, and most significant because of its bearing upon contemporary Europe, is the transformation which has taken place in the minds of the peoples between 1848 and 1914. Thus, the Italians having acquired liberty and unity at the cost of three wars, and sacrifices equally splendid and terrible, lightly embarked upon a programme of national expansion which envisaged, not merely the liberation of the Latin populations of Trieste and the Trentino, but also the forcible annexation of the German of the Upper Adige and the Slavic of Dalmatia.

The Germans, having, after centuries of division, achieved their own unity, promptly shattered that of France by the annexation of Alsace-Lorraine. Nor after 1871 did the mass of this German people see any incongruity in justifying the annexation of Strasbourg, because its inhabitants were Teutonic, and that of Metz, because, despite the fact that all its citizens were French, its forts constituted a fresh guarantee of German security. With equally passionate fervour, too, German patriots proclaimed their right to ethnic unity in the west at the expense of France, and to territorial unity in the east at the cost of Poland.

In the Balkans, the Greeks, the Bulgarians and the Serbs first fell upon the Turks, alike in the name of race and religion, and then upon each other in the attempt to acquire lands which in every case were in part beyond the ethnic limits of the claimant races. The Rumanians, for their part, while continuing to urge their ethnic claims to Bessarabia, Transylvania and the Banat, hastened to despoil the prostrate Bulgarians of the Silistrian strip in which a Latin population was all to seek.

Such was the Europe which a patriotic Serb gunman precipitated into universal conflict. And such was the Europe which emerged from the World War with every racial aspiration and national ambition intensified a thousandfold. In this Europe, peoples had replaced princes in the control of states, but, as they mounted to power, they had adopted the policies of their predecessors. The appetites of monarchs for provinces no longer menaced the tranquillity of the Continent, but between the ambitions of the kings who had vanished, and the peoples who ruled in their stead, the difference was indistinguishable.

Manifestly, then, the history of the century of the rise of democratic nationalism constituted an overwhelming refutation of the Wilsonian assumption that peoples, having come to power, would prove themselves less exigent in the matter of racial and territorial claims than the monarchs whom they had replaced. Nor was the proof less immediate and overwhelming that the destructions and agonies of the War had in no measure modified the ambitions of peoples.

For, on the very threshold of the Paris Conference, the statesmen who were to make peace were assailed by an explosion of discordant and conflicting nationalisms. The French people claimed the left bank of the Rhine in the name of security, and without regard to the rights of the German populations of the Rhineland. The Germans insisted upon the retention of Posen with similar unconcern for the Polish majorities of that province. In the Danubian Plain, the Magyars passionately protested their title to all of their old provinces despite the presence in them of millions of Slavs and Latins. But the Rumanians, the Serbs and the Czechs claimed regions which were purely Hungarian. Even the Belgians, newly released from German occupation, renewed their demands for Dutch territory south of the Scheldt.

Nor was the quarrel limited to disputes between the victors and the vanquished. On the contrary, Poles and Czechs exchanged shots over Teschen and Italians and Serbs came to the very edge of a new conflict over the possession of Fiume. In January, 1919, and in all the following months, the civilized world was filled with the reverberations of the racial quarrels of peoples at Paris.

Instinct in the Wilson conception of the Fourteen Points, too, was still another vital assumption. In the light of the ethnic circumstances of the European Continent, it was inevitable that millions of people should be condemned to live under alien rule. The process of uniting majorities ineluctably imposed the necessity of creating minorities. But, patently, these minorities were bound to be the cause of fresh international disturbance unless their rights were guaranteed by some form of international control. The century-long oppression of their Polish subjects by the Prussians, the familiar tale of the wrongs of the Rumanians and Slavs in Hungary, supplied definitive proof of this certainty.

But, in the secret councils of the Conference, Wilson discovered promptly that no people was prepared to surrender that portion of its national sovereignty necessary to permit international protection of its minorities. For, in the eyes of all peoples, such minorities were not merely a source of domestic incoherence, but inevitably constituted a basis for the claims of neighboring races, to which they belonged ethnically, upon the territory in which they dwelt. Thus, precisely the same considerations that made peoples imperialistic abroad, insured that they would be "hundred percenters" at home.

All the assumptions upon which Wilson had founded his Fourteen Points were, then, equally inexact. Peoples were not less imperialistic than kings, the war had not substituted reason for unrestrained nationalism, and for all races the existence of minorities within their territories was an inevitable urge to undertake forcible assimilation in the interests of national unity and security alike.

In the light of this spirit of democratic nationalism everywhere present, and in the face of the ethnic circumstances of the European Continent, it is therefore manifest that a settlement, satisfactory, or even tolerable in the eyes of all peoples, was totally out of the question. But it is to miss the larger significance of the Paris Conference, itself, and similarly to fail to grasp the vital elements in the problem of post-war peace in Europe, to view this Conference as a time and place where the excessive nationalisms of various peoples—and in fact of the victorious nations—led to the perversion of a principle which was sound in itself, and thus to subsequent international anarchy.

In reality the explanation lies far deeper. Excessive the demands of all peoples were, and similarly, many of the decisions made by the statesmen of 1919 were wholly unjust. Nevertheless, the claims of all peoples, victorious and vanquished alike, were founded upon the desire to acquire or to retain rights which the American people, in their own case, hold to be inherent and therefore inalienable, namely the rights to liberty, unity and security. But because of the ethnic conditions of the European Continent, equal enjoyment of these rights is physically impossible, and this fact constitutes the very heart of the European problem.

The old principle of the balance of power had set the right of Europe as a whole to security, and therefore to peace, above all else. The democratic doctrine, by contrast, made the right of every people to ethnic unity and national security absolute, and thus constituted each people the sole and final judge of its rights. But in a Europe in which races were inextricably entangled, such a doctrine led inescapably to anarchy. The passion and fury with which all peoples pressed claims which were palpably unreasonable, and the unmistakable injustices of the Paris Settlement, itself, long blinded the English speaking world to the fundamental truth. But the slightest examination of the ethnic facts of the European Continent, made in the light of the spirit of democratic nationalism, discloses the double truth that equal enjoyment of national rights is physically impossible, and forcible denial, incompatible with peace.

Chapter Four

ECONOMIC FACTORS

THERE remained also the economic aspect. The Settlement of Vienna had broken down not because the doctrine of the balance of power had been falsified by the Treaty provisions of 1815, but because it was based upon a political principle which became increasingly inapplicable to Nineteenth Century Europe. But was the principle of self determination reconcilable with the economic realities of an industrial age? In a word, could a self-determined Europe be self-supporting?

The three hundred years between the Thirty Years War and the World War were, in European history, marked by the progressive unification of large areas into great states. France, Spain and Britain had become national units in the contemporary sense long before the French Revolution. The unification, first of Italy, and then of Germany, had contributed in the latter half of the Nineteenth Century to the further extinction of minor political units. Seizure of the Eastern shore of the Baltic and

the partitions of Poland had given Russia the dimensions of a world empire. And through the centuries, the Hapsburgs had managed to retain control of a monarchy which in size was the second in
Europe.

The industrial revolution, following in the wake
of this process of territorial integration of states,
had reënforced political by economic bonds. Railway systems, constructed in harmony with national
circumstances, rivers canalized, and ports extended
with similar regard for political conditions, had
completed the transformation. And, in the same
fashion, national industries had been built up on
the basis of national markets. The interdependence
between provinces and cities, industrial areas and
agricultural regions had been established. Customs
barriers about national states had reënforced this
political unity.

Thus, whereas before the French Revolution, the
transfer of a province from one monarch to another
involved a minimum of economic disturbance in a
world where, in the main, all peoples were agricultural and all regions largely self-supporting, similar
changes in 1919 forecast economic revolution and
insured industrial chaos. When, moreover, the extent of the changes to be made amounted, in fact,
to transforming the situation in at least half of the

European Continent, the economic consequences were patently bound to be almost measureless.

Again, to create a new Europe, in accordance with the principle of self-determination, was to reverse the whole process of the centuries, since it necessitated the resolution of great states into their ethnic factors. Moreover, as a first glance at the ethnic map of Europe discloses the impossibility of arriving at clear divisions between peoples, the most cursory examination of the physical indicates the equal impossibility of reconciling racial conditions with geographical, and therefore with economic circumstances.

For it is precisely in those regions which are naturally interdependent and economically bound up together that the ethnic confusion is most complete. In these areas, political frontiers, based on ethnic circumstances, must divide seaports from their hinterlands, agricultural regions which feed cities, from their familiar markets, and the factories of the cities from their rural consumers. Mines must be cut off from nearby industrial plants, towns from the navigable rivers, and as one may discover all over Central Europe today, the farm from the field, the house from the barn, and even the dwelling-place from the highway.

Self-determination, thus applied, must isolate cities which have developed as the ports and the industrial centers of vast regions, or, as the political capitals of large states, and leave them, walled in by customs barriers at their very gates. In the same fashion, countries, self-determined into new and restricted limits, must be condemned to compete in their old markets once within the same customs frontiers. And, inevitably, political considerations will dictate economic regulations without regard to all else.

Thus, to apply the principle of self-determination to the centre of Europe, amounted to passing a sentence of death upon many cities and upon large industrial regions and huge agricultural areas. It involved the dislocation of transportation systems, the neglect of rivers, which once usefully served town and country, alike. It dictated the abandonment of great and costly railway systems, and the expensive and futile construction of new. It insured, not only a break with history and habit but also the abandonment of natural associations and lines of communication for others which accorded only with ethnic details. Old cities were doomed to decay, while new rose to fulfil their ancient functions, visible from their towers, but just beyond national frontiers.

Again, if it was beyond doubt that the resolution of Europe into its ethnic fractions would establish new states, which were bound to prosper, it was not less patent that old nations would be left after mutilation, incapable of maintaining on their restricted area the populations which had concentrated there to fulfil industrial missions, now abolished. But the new political frontiers forbade emigration, and thus dying cities and despairing populations were bound to set grave social problems for Europe as a whole.

Unquestionably the extent of the catastrophe could be limited, if political separation were not permitted to involve economic divorce. But here, again, the precedent was as plain as the subsequent performance proved inevitable. Everywhere on the Continent, political frontiers had been paralleled by formidable tariff walls. But in pre-war Europe, these walls had been of slow development, whereas those which doubled new frontiers must suddenly and violently separate populations whose interdependence was so complete and so traditional that divorce would insure immediate and continuing disaster. Finally, the occasional use of the tariff as a means of coercion or reprisal, notably in the case of Austria and Serbia, similarly foreshadowed fresh disturbances which must now follow the multiplication of frontiers of friction accompanied by the exacerbation of racial feuds.

Thus it is evident that, as the application of the principle of self-determination at Paris could not

produce peace between peoples because of the ethnic conditions, it was predestined to inflict unlimited and incalculable disaster on the whole Continent, because of its economic results. And here the
evil was totally unrelated to the just or unjust allo-
cation of populations and the fair or unfair fixation
of frontiers. Indeed, the decisions which were most
equitable, were not infrequently fraught with the
most fatal consequences. On the economic side, the
rights of people were irreconcilable with their necessities. As the doctrine of the balance of power
had proven an Eighteenth Century precept inapplicable in the Europe of another age, the principle of
self-determination was now disclosed as the political dogma of the Nineteenth Century totally
irrelevant to the economic realities of the
Twentieth.

Viewed, too, in the perspective of less than a
decade and a half, it is already evident that no debate could have been more futile than that which
once raged over two continents as to whether Wilson, Lloyd George and Clemenceau had wickedly,
or only blindly, sacrificed the noble principles of
Democracy to the surviving prejudices of an older
world. For, in fact, even an incomplete application
of these principles at Paris has already resulted in
the economic ruin of half of Europe.

Chapter Five

THE FAILURE OF PARIS

THE Paris Conference, then, failed to provide Europe with a viable system of peace and an adequate foundation of prosperity primarily because of the impossibility of reconciling the ethnic and economic circumstances of the Continent with the principle of self-determination. And, since the inextricable intermingling of races made it inevitable that the rights of certain peoples should be subordinated to those of others, the outcome of the war made it similarly inevitable that the peoples of the Central Powers should suffer. But the defeated nations, also satisfied of the absolute character of their rights, saw in the decisions of Paris only a work of injustice founded upon a military victory.

This view, too, was fortified by the fact that it was possible to find in the territorial, as in all other phases of the treaties, innumerable examples of stupidity resulting from ignorance, and not a few where plain greed was responsible for inequitable decisions. Nevertheless, while, for example, no

35

moral warrant can be discovered for turning the
Austrians of the Southern Tyrol over to Italy, for
the surrender of the Hungarians of the Island of
Schutt to Czecho-Slovakia, for imprisoning the
Germans of Danzig in a free state utterly repugnant to them, none of these wrongs, nor all the
many other perversions of the principle of self-determination, were responsible for the post-war
anarchy.

On the contrary, to restore Meran to Austria
would not affect the question of the Anschluss,
Hungarian irredentism would be little modified by
the recovery of Komarom, and the return of Danzig
to the Reich would leave the Polish Corridor undisturbed and merely insure greater prosperity for
Gdynia, and wider ruin for Danzig. And no misapprehension of the European problem could be
more complete than that which sees peace assured
by the simple process of undoing the patent wrongs
and injustices of the Peace Treaties. For the really
formidable difficulties arise where equal rights are
in collision, and only one of two national solutions
is possible.

Nor is it less unmistakable that in the years since
the making of the Paris Settlement, Europe has suffered at least as severely from economic disintegration, due to an exact application of the doctrine of
self-determination in certain areas, as from political

controversy arising out of actual perversion of this principle in others. In fact, in by far the larger portion of Central Europe it is, today, difficult to determine whether the greater peril for the future arises from the disputes between peoples across new frontiers, or the misery of populations within them.

It is true, as has been incessantly proclaimed, that the Paris Settlement was a peace of force and not of understanding, but in the main, and despite familiar exceptions, that was because the temper of peoples and the circumstances of Europe made amicable adjustment of territorial disputes impossible, and the post-war years have in no way modified this situation.

Since, however, the Paris Settlement was thus necessarily based upon force, the antecedent condition of tranquillity in Europe was that there should be provided adequate force to maintain, at least temporarily, that system of order, which had been created by the peace treaties. But no such force was then or thereafter discoverable.

Woodrow Wilson had sought to give the Paris Settlement those moral guarantees which could flow only from the recognition by all peoples, victorious and vanquished alike, that the peace treaties constituted a just and equitable recognition of their rights. He failed because the physical and psychological obstacles proved equally insurmountable.

Georges Clemenceau had endeavored to provide material guarantees for the structure by the perpetuation of the military alliance, which had won the war. He, too, failed, because the British and American peoples were utterly unwilling to mount guard eternally, not alone on the Rhine, but also on the Vistula, the Danube and the Dniester.

But the double failure to provide the system of Paris with moral, or with material guarantees, was utterly disastrous. A hundred years before, the Congress of Vienna had been able to re-establish peace because, even after nearly a quarter of a century of continuous convulsion, the framework of the old Europe still remained intact. After the fall of Napoleon as before the outbreak of the French Revolution, Austria, Prussia, Russia and Britain continued as they had been.

By contrast, even before the Paris Conference assembled, the pre-war Europe had collapsed in irremediable ruin. The Hapsburg Monarchy had disintegrated; the Romanoff Empire had succumbed to Bolshevism; a domestic revolution had swept away the old order in the Hohenzollern state, and the consequences of defeat were bound to leave Germany powerless for many years. Thus three of the five historically great powers had been either permanently or temporarily removed from the circle of European states.

And, in the place of these great powers, there now appeared at least half a dozen smaller countries either literally recalled from the grave or newly and immeasurably expanded on the fragile foundations of their former insignificance. Europe was, then, suddenly resolved into a chaos of relatively minor states separated, not only by secular rivalries, but also by newly awakened animosities. And while the peoples of western and central Europe were plunged into universal and destructive controversy, beyond the Niemen and the Beresina, Red Russia was preparing a challenge to the whole political and social system of the capitalistic world.

The contrast with the situation in 1815 was in another respect striking and significant. Not alone had the statesmen of Vienna restored order in Europe, but in addition, their collective resources had been adequate thereafter to impose their will upon the Continent, and their recent experiences and individual interests dictated a cooperation after the making of peace as it had compelled association during the war.

Thus, when Napoleon returned from Elba, although the system of Vienna was briefly thrown into confusion, the allies, who had already once overthrown Napoleon, at Waterloo again established the fact of the invincibility of their arms and the solidarity of their coalition. The events of the

Hundred Days, therefore, gave permanence to the structure of the Congress of Vienna, and the force thus disclosed actually insured its endurance for more than four decades thereafter.

By contrast, the arrival of Bela Kun in Budapest, in the winter of 1919, instantly revealed the utter lack of unity or of force surviving in the alliance which had a few months before brought Germany to surrender. Precisely in the same way, half a dozen feeble and futile attempts to break Bolshevist control in Russia, further advertised to the world the impotence of the Allied and Associated Powers. Finally, when a few months after the peace treaties had actually become effective, the approach of the Russian armies to Warsaw disclosed the victors of 1918, not alone without resources to defend the state, which they had re-established, but also, incapable of agreeing, even in principle, to undertake such defense, the last semblance of authority was stripped from them.

After 1815 there had been a Holy Alliance, which had endured for a full generation, and even in 1849, Russian armies had suppressed Hungarian rebellion in the name of the old Austro-Russian association of 1814-15. After the long series of national wars ending in the Franco-Prussian conflict, a Concert of Europe had re-appeared at the Congress of Berlin. As late as the winter of 1913, a

Council of Ambassadors, representing at least a fiction of a united Europe had liquidated the First Balkan War in the interests of general tranquillity and, by virtue of the authority resident in great powers, acting in unison.

But the World War had abolished the last remaining vestiges of authority and unity on the European Continent. Kings, courts, all the resources of old fashioned diplomacy, all the traditions of international association had been swept away. And in the place of the familiar machinery of diplomatic intercourse, nothing had been substituted save the grotesque improvisation of international conferences (of which that of Paris was the first) attended only by national politicians dependent for their political existence upon fulfilling the national will of their respective peoples. And in such conferences, the impossibility of reconciling the conflicting national purposes of peoples was invariably disclosed.

In the destruction of the Old Europe, the role of the Anglo-Saxon peoples had been decisive. They had intervened in a Continental war, which in its immediate origin and issues was without relation to themselves, for reasons which were exclusively national. Thus, the British had been concerned for their naval security, the Americans for their maritime rights. The effect of this intervention had been to enable one group of European peoples to defeat another. But while the fact of victory, by insuring the annihilation of German seapower, constituted the fulfilment of the purposes of the Anglo-Saxon nations, victory for their European allies was meaningless save as the peace settlement insured the realization of the war aims for which they had been fighting.

By contrast, not only were the Anglo-Saxon peoples utterly uninterested in the realization of these war aims, but they soon discovered in the terms proposed by their Continental associates a menace either to their political interests or to their material welfare. For them the deadly enemy of yesterday had become the prospective customer of tomorrow. Considerations of trade, commerce and finance, all moved them to seek the speedy restoration of Germany, and to oppose all the projects of their recent associates which tended to prevent or postpone such recovery, and thus, in their view, to continue the war.

In a word, the Anglo-Saxon peoples asserted that their right to a tranquil Europe and a Germany made safe for business was absolute and, as a consequence, that the programme of the victorious Continental peoples, formulated with the purpose of insuring the security of nations which had recently been invaded, or long divided and forcibly partitioned, must be subordinated to British and American interests. Woodrow Wilson, to be sure, had promised the French a treaty of guarantee in return for their abandonment of their own programme of security at the Rhine, but the American Senate rejected this compromise because it patently did violence to the American tradition of isolation and the American people, in their turn, presently adopted the view of their Senate.

Thus, while on the one hand, the text of the treaties actually framed at Paris, seemed to the defeated peoples, who were compelled to surrender populations and territories, a wicked and intolerable denial of their rights, the attitude of the Anglo-Saxon powers filled them with hope that revision of the system of Paris would prove, not only possible, but inevitable. Precisely in the same fashion, however, the policy of the Anglo-Saxon peoples and the undisguised purposes of the recently defeated states, filled the minds of the victorious and Succession peoples with a sense of insecurity, which led them to maintain vast military establishments and to indulge in acts of violence, like the occupation of Budapest, and of the Ruhr, little distinguishable from war itself, and totally destructive of the atmosphere of calm and confidence essential to Anglo-Saxon business.

The failure of Paris was, then, twofold. Between

the Continental peoples recently at war, no adjustment of conflicting ethnic and territorial rights proved possible. And, in the same way, no compromise between the programmes of peace of the Anglo-Saxon peoples and their Continental associates, was discoverable. In both cases, this failure was due to the same conviction in the minds of each individual people that its own rights were absolute. But while the absence of agreement between the Continental peoples inevitably gave the Paris Settlement the character of a peace of violence and not of understanding, the break between the Anglo-Saxon and Continental peoples, who had made the war together, deprived the peace treaties of the necessary force to insure their endurance—at least for a time sufficient to allow Europe to recover morally and economically from the ruin of the recent war.

Therefore, while the Armistice of Rethondes terminated the actual fighting of the World War and the Treaties of Paris legally terminated the conflict, the collision between the wills of peoples continued thereafter uninterruptedly. Nor could there be any grimmer paradox than that disclosed in the fact that, while following pathways which led inescapably to new conflict, European peoples still asserted that another war would mean the extinction of civilization itself.

PART TWO

TERRITORIAL ISSUES

Chapter Six

STATUS QUO AND REVISION

THE failure of the Paris Conference inevitably bestowed upon Europe the evil inheritance of many territorial disputes. In fact, it insured the continuation of the divisions of the war, itself. The peoples whose frontiers had been mutilated and provinces partitioned now demanded the revision of the peace treaties, while those who had attained liberty, unity or security, insisted upon the preservation of the status quo. And the clash of these purposes prevented the reconciliation of peoples, and postponed the return of the Continent to normal conditions.

For the American, like the British people, this new state of anarchy on the Continent was at once inexplicable and intolerable. In their eyes, the World War, which had cost them dearly in blood and treasure, had been caused by similar rivalries. With amazement and indignation they had watched the Peace Conference degenerate into a battle for the possession of provinces and cities. Now, al-

though the peace treaties put a legal term to conflict, it was the chaos of the old Europe, not the
tranquillity of a new, which confronted them. The
war which they had proclaimed was to end war
seemed to have become only a prelude to the next.

Inescapably this European chaos aroused bitter
resentment in the minds of both Anglo-Saxon peoples. Both, with equal clarity, perceived the consequences, but for both, the territorial issues involved
were similarly meaningless. And since the issues
were meaningless, the passions which they provoked
were incomprehensible. Neither the American nor
the British peoples had in their remembered experience either invasion during war or partition
after defeat. As a consequence, the emotions of
other peoples, who had recently suffered both,
awakened no sympathetic understanding in Washington or London.

Since they were unable to understand the issues
involved or the passion aroused by these territorial
disputes, the Anglo-Saxon peoples easily and simply classified the new quarrels with the old. They
discovered in both proof of the existence amongst
the European peoples of ambitions, passions, emotions which had no counterpart in their own lives.
Imperialism, militarism and chauvinism were employed alike as terms of identification and of condemnation. And the conviction took root that at

heart all European peoples hid beneath an outward pretense of devotion to peace an instinctive fondness for war.

At bottom, this interpretation, at once cruel and unjust, had its origin in the fact that for both the British and the American peoples, the territorial issues seemed only territorial; were for them no more than incredible quarrels over relatively insignificant parcels of real estate. But, in point of fact, for the peoples actually in controversy, the issue was always primarily one of human beings, and not of land. Thus, for the Poles and Germans, the question of the Polish Corridor is above and beyond all else an issue which involves the fate of hundreds of thousands of men and women dwelling in and about the contested area, who belong to their race, speak their tongue and claim their protection.

For the Anglo-Saxons, on the contrary, the Polish Corridor has no concrete meaning. At most, it is only a splash of color on the map of Europe. It is a remote and obscure tract of land on an unfamiliar continent. That two peoples, presumably civilized, should be willing in order to hold or regain this land, to risk a war fraught with disaster for the contestants and ruin for the Continent, seems proof of the utter madness of Polish and German nationalism, alike.

Almost never do British or American critics of

German and Polish policies, in respect of the Corridor, attempt to translate these European issues into the political circumstances of their own lives. Thus Americans, who in the name of world peace, unhesitatingly demand German or Polish sacrifice in the matter of the Corridor, would be astounded at the mere suggestion that the United States should cede New England to Canada or California to Mexico. Yet the sacrifice would not be disproportionate to that which they require of the Continental peoples. Similarly, Americans, who would regard it as a piece of unimaginable impertinence for a European public opinion to demand international protection of the political rights of the Negro majorities in various Southern States, solemnly urge such protection for the rights of minorities within various national frontiers in Europe.

In the same fashion, Britons, for whom the configuration of the Corridor seems preposterous in itself and fantastic, because it destroys German unity, remain totally unaware of the appearance to all alien eyes of the frontiers drawn in Ireland at the expense of Irish unity. And the Protestant minority in Ulster is far smaller than the Polish in prewar West Prussia. Nor does concern for German minorities in Pomerelia or Upper Silesia extend to similar disquiet about the wrongs of the Catholic majorities in Tyrone and Fermanagh.

Yet the beginning of any understanding of the European problem must be predicated upon the perception of the fact that, while quarrels between peoples nominally concern territory, they are serious chiefly because they affect human beings. It is because status quo and revision equally involve condemning vast masses of human beings to conditions as intolerable for them as life under French Canadian or Latin-American rule would be for citizens of the United States, or under Irish Free State sovereignty, for the Protestants of Northern Ireland, that peoples, who know from recent experience what war means, place their territorial claims above peace itself. For innumerable centuries mankind has celebrated the wisdom of Solomon in the case of claimant mothers. But the horror of the knife disclosed by the authentic mother in that, perhaps the first partition treaty of which history has a record, is still revealed in all the territorial issues of the Continent.

There is yet another cause of misapprehension in Anglo-Saxon minds and that arises from the reparations and disarmament provisions of the peace treaties. American and British publics are satisfied that the money payments required of Germany are beyond her capacity to pay. They recognize, also, that the unilateral disarmament conditions impose a state of intolerable helplessness upon a great people disarmed in the midst of an armed Europe. What, however, they see less clearly is that insistence by the Status Quo states upon these terms arises, not from the purpose or desire to keep the defeated peoples forever impoverished and defenseless, but solely to obtain from them a renunciation of their programme of territorial revision.

Had the peoples seeking territorial amendments renounced these purposes, the whole framework of impossible payments and inequitable disarmament conditions would have been modified long ago. On the other hand, were the nations now held disarmed and to ransom, able to regain their material prosperity and their former military strength without renouncing their territorial objectives, their power to realize these purposes would be absolute and the ruin of the Status Quo peoples inevitable.

Actually, therefore, for Status Quo and Revision peoples, alike, the struggle over reparations and armaments has been identified with equal clarity as a skirmish, preliminary to the main battle over the territorial issues. On both sides reparations and armaments are viewed as the outworks of the system of 1919, and the territorial circumstances, as the inner citadel. Thus the Status Quo powers have defended the outworks with an energy commensurate with their concern for the main fortress; while the Revision peoples have returned to the assault of the front line trenches again and again, with the same clear perception of their ultimate objective.

The Anglo-Saxon peoples, on the contrary, have seen only the economic ruin resulting from the conflict and the inherent folly of both the reparations and armament details of the treaties. They have labored to bring about the abolition of both with utter unconcern for the consequences to the unity and security of the Status Quo peoples. But they have never undertaken to promote a parallel modification of the purposes of the Revision peoples. Nor have they ever proffered their own guarantees to the peoples plainly menaced by the economic recovery of states resolved upon territorial revision.

The result has been failure, deadlock and continued economic and financial disintegration. Yet it is, of course, absurd to imagine that these consequences have passed unperceived by the eyes of the nations at odds over territorial issues. On the contrary, these consequences have been identified with utmost clarity. It is the Anglo-Saxon peoples who have failed to grasp the meaning to the people directly involved, of the only discoverable alternative. Ignorance of the actual character of the territorial issues themselves, has obscured the reasons why they appear matters of life and death for the Status Quo and Revision peoples, alike.

To understand this state of mind, the consequences of which have dominated all the post-war history of Europe, it is necessary, therefore, to examine these territorial issues, themselves. And beyond all else, it is necessary to see them in the eyes of peoples who are risking their own existence and imperilling the peace of the world by policies, which have their origin in these disputes.

Chapter Seven

THE POLISH CORRIDOR

OF THE Polish Corridor, it might be said with exactitude that it is an encyclopedia of the ills of contemporary Europe. In it are illustrated all the disputes, historical, ethnic, religious, and economic, which are otherwise discoverable separately from Hel to the Golden Horn. Moreover, in this dispute one finds, not alone the reason for the enduring feud between the German and Polish peoples, but also for the failure of many attempts at reconciliation between the German and French, as well. In a word, the Corridor has replaced Belgium as the "cockpit" of Europe.

Geographically, the limits of the Corridor are hard to fix, for the simple reason that the Germans, themselves, have never set a definitive limit to the territory which they claim. In practice, however, it is generally understood to include the present Polish province of Pomerelia and the Netze district, belonging to the adjoining province of Posen, that is, the territory taken by Prussia in the first Partition of Poland, together with the district now included in the Danzig Free State. Thus delimited, it has an area roughly equal to that of Massachusetts and Connecticut combined, and a population of somewhat less than a million and a half.

Historically, this region has been the battleground of Slav and Teuton for more than seven centuries. The struggle began when a Polish Duke of Mazovia invited the Teutonic Knights to establish themselves on the east bank of the Vistula and to undertake the task of conquering and converting the pagan Prussians, who were troubling his borders. This was in 1225, and during the following hundred years the Teutonic Knights established themselves in all the region between the Niemen and the Vistula. They covered their territory with enormous castles, many of which survive as monuments to their builders and as rivals in brick of the more famous structures on the Rhine. At Marienburg on the Nogat, their capital, they erected a fortress still deserving its title of the Carcassonne of the North.

Once established, however, the Teutonic Order waged war equally with Pole and Prussian. The latter were presently either assimilated or annihilated, and thousands of colonists were brought from South Germany to settle this wilderness. In the fourteenth century, the Order crossed the Vistula and repeated its exploits. Here again, conquest was followed by colonization. Henceforth, therefore, the population on this left bank of the Vistula was mixed, while Danzig became, what it has always remained, a purely Teutonic town. In the fifteenth century, however, the Poles defeated the Teutonic Knights at Tannenberg, on the same field where five hundred years later Hindenburg won his great victory over the Russians. Thereafter, the disintegration of the Order was rapid, and the Second Treaty of Thorn in 1466 not only restored the west bank of the Vistula to Poland, along with Danzig, but transformed the Grand Master of the Order into a vassal of the Polish Throne for the East Prussian Duchy.

In the eighteenth century, Frederick the Great found himself possessed of this Prussian Duchy, which had passed to the Electors of Brandenburg, and had thus escaped from Polish suzerainty, but was still separated from his other dominions by the Polish Corridor, erected by the Treaty of Thorn. To abolish this Corridor and establish territorial unity for his kingdom, he engineered the First Partition of Poland. The Second and Third extended Prussian holdings of Polish territory, and even Napoleon, in creating his short-lived Grand Duchy of Warsaw, refrained from restoring the

Corridor. Finally, the Congress of Vienna confirmed Prussian title to the Corridor, now become West Prussia, and to Posen as well, and this condition endured thereafter until the close of the World War.

On the historical side, it is clear, therefore, that, while the Poles base their claim upon original possession and three centuries of undisturbed occupation between 1466 and 1772, the Germans rest their title upon the conquest and colonization by the Knights, and upon the century and a half of possession between 1772 and 1919. Ethnically, the situation is even more intricate as a consequence of the long centuries of intermingling. That the territory was originally inhabited by Slavs before the advent of the Teutonic Order seems certain. That before the World War East Prussia was largely Germanized and West Prussia partially, is equally true.

In 1919, that is, at the moment of the making of the Treaty of Versailles, the situation was confused. In fact, all depended upon the area chosen for a test. Thus, in the whole province of West Prussia and the Netze District, there was an undoubted German majority. In the region actually taken from Germany, that is, the Corridor and the Danzig Free State, while the margin was much narrower, the German advantage was still probably decisive. On

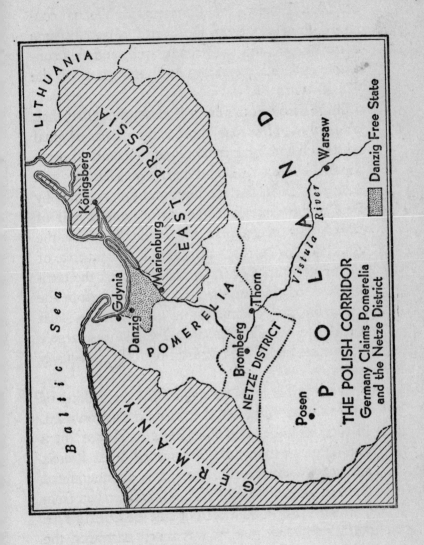

LITHUANIA

EAST PRUSSIA

Königsberg

Marienburg

Baltic Sea

Gdynia

Danzig

POMERELIA

GERMANY

Bromberg

NETZE DISTRICT

Thorn

Posen

POLAND

Vistula River

Warsaw

Danzig Free State

THE POLISH CORRIDOR
Germany Claims Pomerelia
and the Netze District

the other hand, in the area actually transferred to Poland, the Slavs quite as certainly, outnumbered the Teutons. But even here, the Germans claim, with justice, that not all the Slavs are Poles, and, with far less warrant, that the Kashubes, living in the Tuchola Heath and farther north, cannot fairly be credited to their rivals.

These claims and counter claims remain somewhat hazy, because they are based on the German side on Prussian statistics, which were notoriously partial and no plebiscite ever took place. The absence of a vote was explained by Wilson's decision to bestow upon Poland access to the sea over her own territory. To give effect to this decision, involved restoring the Corridor as it had existed before the First Partition. Wilson's decision was, too, based upon the obvious fact that the new Poland would have an area greater than that of Italy and a population in excess of the Spanish, and without free access to the sea, this large area and great population would be economically at the mercy of Germany, which would hold its natural sea gates. Wilson, too, was profoundly influenced by what he conceived to be the moral issue involved in undoing the work of the Partitions.

Poland, without Danzig, would be the situation of that part of America between the Alleghanies and the Rockies, in the period when France was still seated at New Orleans. For the relation of the Vistula to all Poland is that of the Mississippi to the great central region of the United States. On the other hand, in German eyes, to erect the Corridor, with its Danzig attachment, necessarily took precisely the form the project to carve out a Canadian Corridor along the Hudson, and erect a New York Free State at the southern extremity, would have in American. And the situation of New England in the latter scheme, would be identical with that of East Prussia, in the former.

As to Danzig City, itself, the free state solution was in accordance with the traditions of this ancient Hanseatic city, and consistent with the ethnic rights of the population, which was almost entirely German. In the old Poland, Danzig had at one time preserved its Teutonic character and its loyalty to the Polish kings. Indeed, even as late as 1815, it had protested against final incorporation in Prussia. Wilson and his associates at Paris could, therefore, believe that history would repeat itself and material interests outweigh ethnic circumstances, but, believing this, they entirely miscalculated the contemporary force of racial sympathies.

The immediate effect of the cession of West Prussia and the Netze District to Poland was threefold. Two million and a quarter of Germans living beyond the Vistula were cut off from the Reich.

Another third of a million were shut up in the Danzig Free State, politically independent but economically bound up with the Poles. Finally, at least half a million more Germans were turned over outright to Polish rule.

To justify such mutilation of Prussian unity in the name of history constituted for Germans just what for Americans would be the retrocession of Southern California to Mexico, or the Far West to the Indians, on the ground that both regions had been taken by violence, and without regard for the ethnic or other rights of the original owners. Moreover, since the Germans held the Poles in the same low esteem the Americans of the West hold both the Mexicans and the Indians, the resentment of a settlement which surrendered half a million Germans to the rule of a race held inferior, is easily to be conjectured. And religious prejudices intensified ethnic hatreds.

German resentment provoked by the loss of West Prussia was further intensified by the subsequent fate of Upper Silesia. Historically, Silesia had been lost to Poland for at least five centuries, passing first to Austria and then to Prussia, following the conquest by Frederick the Great. Until the second half of the Nineteenth Century, however, the population had remained Slavic and the region purely agricultural.

But discovery of vast coal deposits had later resulted in the transformation of Upper Silesia into the second greatest industrial area of the German Empire. German technical skill and German capital had combined to develop the region. The Oder had been canalized to provide cheap transportation to the Baltic, and Stettin, at its mouth, had become a great port. In Upper Silesia, itself, cities had risen in which the population was largely German, while along with industrialization, assimilation had progressed in the Slavic portion of the population.

To surrender this region to Poland because of a disputable ethnic circumstance, was for all Germans as preposterous as would be for the present masters of Pittsburgh, the necessity to restore their district to the Algonquins—if any still survive. Nor did the later decision to divide an area which was economically indissoluble to suit racial conditions, appear less fantastic.

Yet here, again, Wilson's intervention determined the outcome. He had at first resolved on the basis of the Slavic character of a majority of the population to demand the unconditional cession of the whole area. British opposition, however, finally imposed a plebiscite. But when the vote was taken, the result only produced fresh controversy because of the terms of the election. Thus, while the Germans polled sixty per cent of the million and a quarter votes cast, the Poles obtained majorities in certain areas, and it had been determined in advance that territorial distribution was to follow the results in localities.

After long and violent discussion, the League of Nations was finally charged with the duty of settling the question, and its decision, as was inevitable in the premises, resulted in a division of the province. The division involved the cession to Poland of the larger portion of the coal deposits and of most of the industrial districts. Cities, too, which had voted for Germany, were inescapably included in the Polish area because of the counterbalancing majorities in their environs. Here, too, as in West Prussia, the Germans based their protests against the decision on the fact of an undeniable Teutonic majority in the whole province, while the Poles rested their claims upon the equally clear presence of a Polish majority in the area actually acquired. Moreover, as the Germans had seen in the erection of the Corridor, the destruction of their territorial unity, they now discovered in the Upper Silesian decision, a similar mutilation of their economic unity.

But far more important than the first emotions stirred by the application of the decisions of the Treaty of Versailles, were those evoked by the later consequences. First of all, throughout all the regions turned over to Poland, there began a vast migration of Germans. Officials, civil servants, soldiers, then bankers, doctors, lawyers, who served these, then the merchant, the grocer, all those dependent upon German custom, took the long road to exile. Expropriation of rural property, accompanied by extensive voluntary sales, swelled the migratory horde. In the first years, more than half a million Germans, (750,000, if German figures are to be accepted) left the eastern marches forever.

And, on the heels of these emigrants, there flowed in an even larger number of Slavic settlers, thousands coming from the Westphalian mines in Germany and more thousands fleeing from the Bolshevist fury in the Ukraine. German frontier cities, even Berlin, now distant but a hundred miles from the new frontier, were compelled to give shelter and find support for the fugitives from the lost battle of Germanism in the east. Almost over night, the German numbers in Posen and Pomerelia melted. Bromberg in the former province, which had counted but 10,000 Poles in 90,000 inhabitants in 1910, retained but 9,000 Germans in 119,000 citizens by 1930. Thorn in the latter province, which had held but 5,000 Poles among its 40,000 residents, now had but 4,000 Germans in 50,000.

Belatedly, too, the Germans at last perceived that the restored Poland had become a permanent fact. So sure had they been when the terms of the Treaty of Versailles had first been published, that Poland was a "Season State" destined to disappear in a few months as a consequence of the utter incapacity of its people to organize a national existence, that thousands of the first exiles had waited at the new frontier for the signal to return. So confident had been the authorities of the Reich of the same event, that despite Polish requests, they had recalled all their local servants and railway operatives, seeking to hasten the collapse. But, after a decade, Polish administration functioned, Polish railways "ran", while German exiles still waited, and the hastily recalled servants now lived by official dole, a permanent burden on the national treasury.

As Poland daily assumed an appearance of stability, as, contrary to every preconceived German judgment, its persistence came to appear more certain, the problem of the eastern frontiers took on an entirely different aspect. It was no longer simply the question of the recovery of the areas actually ceded, but more poignantly the problem of the retention of regions which were still German; of Danzig, which, as a free state, maintained its German character and of East Prussia, now become an ethnic island beyond the German frontiers.

As for Danzig, while the local government, by

means of property and citizenship laws, still arrested Polish infiltration, its refusal to enter into
the life of Poland, accentuated by an interference,
which nearly prevented the passage of arms and
munitions when the Bolshevist armies were at the
gates of Warsaw, had led to the creation on Polish
soil of the new port of Gdynia. And this new port
had arisen from a fishing village of 200 inhabitants to a city of 45,000 in less than a decade.
Equipped with new machinery and with modern
docks, fed by a railway, constructed by French capital, and offering shorter, and therefore cheaper
transportation for Silesian coal than the old route
via Danzig, it now became a deadly rival. Month
by month, while the tonnage of Danzig remained
stationary, that of Gdynia took on new proportions.

Thus, in fact, Germanism within Danzig is not
only undergoing siege, but is actually *in extremis.*
At will, the Poles can shut off the flow of coal
cargoes and complete a ruin which had begun when
separation from the Reich paralyzed all local industries. A day may come when the price for the
commerce by which it lives will be demanded in
the shape of the suppression of laws which exclude
Poles from citizenship. But, on the next day, the
flow of Polish immigration is sure to repeat the
Polonization which had already taken place in

Bromberg, become Bydgoszcz, and Thorn, which is now Torun.

As to East Prussia, isolated from the Reich, and on the military side entirely defenseless, since all new fortification is forbidden by the Treaty of Versailles, even before the war, it had been a land of emigration in which the natural increase of population was overbalanced by the flow to Berlin and Westphalia. Always its great estates had been farmed solely by the employment of Polish labour. But in later years, while the world-wide economic depression produced acute crisis, at its frontiers there has been waiting a flood of Polish peasants, land-hungry, and not only eager to take up the land, become unprofitable for German cultivation, but also capable of prospering on it because of their lower standard of living.

Immediately after the Treaty of Versailles took effect, land communications between the Reich and East Prussia were bad. The Poles exploited their control of the connecting railways in such fashion as to hamper the transit of goods and humiliate the German passengers. In later years, all these abuses have been terminated and today the flow of goods is as cheap and efficient as before the war, and travellers are undisturbed. But the power to revert to the earlier manner remains with the Poles, and the fear of such reversion is a continuing element of uncertainty in German minds.

To the Germans, therefore, not alone the fate of Danzig, but also that of East Prussia now seems in the balance. Despite nationalistic protests, however, this danger does not arise from any prospect of Polish aggression. On the contrary, time is working too advantageously for the Poles to permit any thought of military adventure. But, by contrast, to nourish this losing battle in the east, the German government is compelled to make ever-increasing drafts upon a treasury already overburdened by reparation payments.

Thus, although in theory, Poland and Germany are at peace today, in fact, a state of war exists everywhere from Danzig to Kattowitz. To visit any of the cities or regions on this battlefront, is to revive the memories of old trips to the firing-lines of the World War. There is no way of translating to the publics of the western world any conception of the passion, agony, misery and fear which exist in all this region, or the effect upon the young generation of a life lived in this atmosphere of hate and apprehension.

Across these new frontiers, too, the politicians of the two countries exchange threats. On the German side, a Cabinet Minister proclaims the inevitability of revision, and on the Polish, new efforts are provoked to complete the extinction of that German minority which serves as an excuse for treaty revision claims. But in this eternal struggle, it is the stronger which is losing, and the weaker which is winning, measured by the numbers and wealth of the two nations. It is, too, the race which has long believed itself superior which is losing in this new war of attrition. But if the evidence of victory gives fresh inspiration to the Poles, the growing perception of ultimate consequences of defeat similarly urges the Germans to greater effort.

Chapter Eight

THE ANSCHLUSS

IF, ON the territorial side, the liquidation of the Hapsburg Monarchy constituted the most considerable task of the Paris Conference, historically it amounted to a revolution. Indeed, to organize Europe without an Austrian Empire, was to undertake a task without precedent in the face of difficulties that were beyond exaggeration. "If Austria did not exist, it would be necessary to invent it," Palacky had once said, and the phrase had lived.

Despite all mutations of centuries, Francis Joseph had been the heir to an unbroken succession remounting to the origin of the Holy Roman Empire, and Vienna possessed an imperial tradition almost as long-continued as that of Rome, itself. Not only did the Austrian tradition descend from remote centuries, but it was also a German tradition. If, by contrast with the Italian, French and British peoples, the German had never succeeded in achieving an enduring political union based upon the inclusion of the Teutonic race within a single system

of frontiers, it had long retained a vital sense of
cultural and moral unity. Divided by a political
particularism, which has been proverbial, the Germans have always felt themselves to be one people.

The Wars of the Reformation, and the quarrels
of the Hapsburgs and Hohenzollerns never, before
1848, served to destroy this sense of racial unity and
it was not, in fact, until 1866, when Bismarck thrust
Austria out of North Germany and, indeed, not
until 1871, when he launched his new German Empire on the flood tide of the victory over France,
that the separation of the Germans of the Hapsburg
Monarachy from those of the new Hohenzollern
Empire, seemed definitive. Thereafter, for half a
century, the world, Teutonic and non-German alike,
forgot in the fact of the ever-growing power and
prestige of the new German Empire, the ancient
and almost legendary tale of an earlier unity of the
German race within more spacious limits.

As the Twentieth Century opened and the centrif-
ugal purposes of the several races in the Austro-
Hungarian Empire became more and more
unmistakable, there appeared concomitantly the
propaganda of a pan-Germanism which aimed at
the reunion of all branches of the Teutonic race
within the framework of the Hohenzollern Empire.
On the whole, this agitation gained few recruits in
Vienna, while the old Dual Monarchy survived,

and served rather to intensify, than to diminish, the secular rivalry between the Hapsburg and Hohenzollern dynasties.

When, however, at the close of the World War, both dynasties crashed, the primary obstacle to union similarly disappeared. When, too, the peace treaties not alone destroyed the old Austro-Hungarian Monarchy, but also separated the German-speaking population of the Austrian half, transferring a third of the ten millions belonging to the Teutonic race to the new Czecho-Slovakian state, and confining the rest within the narrow limits of an Austrian Republic, it was inevitable that both fractions should instinctively seek not a reunion in a national state, which would still be insignificant, but inclusion within the frontiers of the German Republic.

In respect of the Austrian Republic, which they undertook to construct, it is clear that the statesmen of Paris were at least influenced by the example of Belgium. When in 1830, the Belgian people had risen against the Dutch, they had offered themselves to France. Not only was such a union ethnically natural, since nearly half, and that the ruling Walloon fraction, were French by race, but also between 1795 and 1814 both Walloons and Flemings had lived within French frontiers.

The union of Belgium with France in 1830

North Sea

Baltic Sea

Danzig

CORRIDOR

EAST
PRUSSIA

Hamburg

POLAND

Berlin

G E R M A N Y

HOLLAND

BELGIUM

FRANCE

Prague

CZECHO-SLOVAKIA

Vienna

AUSTRIA

SWITZERLAND

S. TYROL

Budapest

HUNGARY

I T A L Y

Trieste

Fiume

YUGO-SLAVIA

THE ANSCHLUSS
Czecho-Slovakia would become
a Slavic Cape Cod in a
German Sea

Adriatic
Sea

Pola

would, however, have destroyed the balance of power in Europe, and thus have completely undone the work of the Congress of Vienna. Therefore Europe, led by Britain, intervened to prevent this expansion of French territory and population, and the Belgian Kingdom was presently established. Before the World War, as since, the quarrels of the two races have complicated the domestic politics of the little state, but in 1914 the German invaders found a united nation in arms against them.

Was it not reasonable to calculate that time would work a similar change on the banks of the Danube? If, beyond debate, to veto the Austrian demand for union with Germany, constituted a denial of the will of the people of this fragment of the old Hapsburg domain, similar denial of the request of the Belgian people had not created an enduring resentment. Was it not possible, even probable, that a similar evolution might take place in popular feeling and render not alone tolerable, but even satisfactory, what at the moment appeared unjust?

On the surface, there were many reasons to warrant such a calculation. Union with the Reich would inevitably reduce Austria to the level of Wurtemburg or Saxony, and Vienna to the rank of provincial capital, like Munich or Dresden. For all Austrians it would mean the sacrifice of one of the oldest and proudest traditions in Europe for a position of political insignificance and economic dependence. And if the makers of the Treaty of St. Germain did not count too much upon the parochial patriotism of the Austrian people, they did rely upon the pride of those who had for so long constituted the ruling race in a great empire.

What the statesmen of Paris did not reckon with, however, was the economic factor. They failed utterly to perceive the material circumstances to which they were condemning the people of Austria, and therefore to foresee the possibility that all other considerations would count for little in the minds of a people at once economically miserable and politically defenseless. But in this state of mind lies the basic explanation of the contemporary demand of the Austrians for the Anschluss.

It is, moreover, to misunderstand completely the Austrian sentiment, in the matter of union with Germany, to identify it with the passion of the French people of Annexed Lorraine for re-union with France after 1870, or of the people of Venice for union with Italy before 1866. The denial of the right of the Austrian people to enjoy the blessings of self-determination convicted the authors of the Paris Settlement of 1919 of a complete disregard of their own principles and professions, but the subsequent demand of the Austrian people for a revision

of the Treaty of St. Germain was almost exclusively
due to material, and not to moral considerations.

The Paris notion to construct a second Belgium,
this time in Central Europe, was ill-conceived because of the absolute difference in the fundamental
conditions of Belgium in 1830 and of Austria in
1919. Alike under Spanish and Austrian rule, the
Netherlands, before the French Revolution, had
enjoyed a semblance of national life, and Brussels
had boasted a minor court. Thus the creation of an
independent Belgian Kingdom represented the extension of a tradition, rather than a violent break
with the past. Swiftly, too, the acquisition of independence was followed by industrial and commercial development. Brussels, Liège, Antwerp took on
new importance, and prosperity was general. The
Belgian who had been, in a certain measure, the
political serf of Spanish, Austrian and Dutch masters, in turn, and the cannon fodder of the Napoleonic Empire, found himself materially, morally,
politically advantaged by his independence.

In the case of Austria, the situation was exactly
the reverse. Almost overnight, the dominant fraction of a mighty empire fell to the estate of another
Switzerland. But, while for the whole country, the
descent was humiliating, for the capital, the economic consequences of the change were catastrophic. For centuries this city, now containing

two millions of inhabitants, had lived upon the trade, commerce, industry and administration of a vast empire. In fact, all of Central and Southeastern Europe had paid tribute to the capital of the Hapsburgs, and for the huge population of this area it had fulfilled the rôles of London and Paris alike.

By the Treaty of St. Germain, however, it was left the capital of a poor mountain state counting but four millions of inhabitants outside the city limits. It had also become a frontier town, encircled on three sides by alien territory, less than an hour distant by train or motor. And this surrounding circle of frontiers was also marked by tariff barriers excluding Vienna from the markets which it had supplied, and the trade and commerce on which its prosperity was founded. It was as if New York City had been reduced to the condition of the port of a politically independent Empire State, and saw its activities limited to serving the exiguous requirements of the peoples of the upstate districts, and its trade and commerce halted at the New Jersey and Connecticut boundaries by customs barriers.

Thus, inevitably, in the post-war years, Vienna has declined, the city which in the splendor of its public buildings rivalled ancient Rome, and in the charm of its life, challenged pre-war Paris, has become the centre of misery and decay beyond exaggeration, and hardly paralleled in contemporary Europe. Commerce has well nigh disappeared, trade has worsened progressively, the great banks which served a quarter of a continent have failed and fallen, one by one. The Socialist majority which dominates the town has waged class war against the old aristocracy and while the city budget has been overweighted to provide magnificent quarters for the proletariat, the old land owners have literally starved within the shadow of their properties, from which they are forbidden by law to draw reasonable rent.

The city limits are, too, a political frontier between metropolitan and rural Austria, and the limit on the one side of a Socialist paradise, and on the other, of a bourgeois society. Riots within the city have more than once nearly brought city and country to blows. But while the municipal population seeks union with Germany to achieve fusion with the Social Democratic party of the Reich, the rural sees in the Anschluss the promise of the protection of the bourgeois parties from the excesses of socialism.

The inevitable drift toward Anschluss in the post-war years has been greatly accentuated by the policy and performances of Fascist Italy. By the Treaty of St. Germain, the Austrians were compelled to surrender to Italy at least a quarter of a million of German-Speaking Tyrolese in the upper valleys of the Adige that the Italians might have their strategic frontier at the Brenner. This decision of the Paris Peace Conference was, and remains, one of the monuments to the triumph of expediency over principle in the Paris Settlement.

With the arrival of Fascism in Italy, this German minority was exposed to one of the most ferocious and far reaching campaigns of forcible assimilation known in post-war Europe. When, too, the protests of the persecuted people reached Vienna, and awakened expressions of indignation and sympathy, these were met in turn by threats of Italian military occupation of Klagenfurt, Innsbruck, and even of Vienna, itself. And the menace of foreign invasion has thus served to reinforce the desire for union with the German Reich, born of economic misery and domestic political insecurity.

In sum, the experiment of an Austrian Republic had demonstrably failed even before the great financial depression of 1931 came to complete the ruin, at once economic and financial, which had been wrought by the earlier years. In those years, financial aid extended through the League of Nations and acompanied by alien supervision, had proven inadequate, while frantic efforts of interested states to establish tariff associations, as a barrier to the Anschluss, had been without avail in arresting that process of disintegration and decay which had set in with the application of the Treaty of St. Germain.

With the passing of years, Austria has thus assumed the rôle of the mendicant among the nations, and Vienna has become the saddest corner of a stricken Continent. To wander through its palaces and parks, is to recapture something of the impression of those who saw Rome after the Cæsars and the first barbarian invaders had both departed, and the imperial monuments, still undisturbed, testified to a greatness which had vanished. Physically the city lives; intellectually, morally, politically, above all spiritually, it is dead. And those who loved it in the pre-war days, visit it now as a tomb. More and more it has become clear that the authors of the Paris Settlement reckoned without the Austrian people themselves. And like an invalid attacked by an illness his physicians do not deem mortal, Austria, lacking the will to live, has defied the best efforts of the doctors.

But while Austria has declined steadily, and Vienna died a little each day, and the demand of the people living alike in city and country for union with the Reich, has increased, the opposition of the neighboring peoples has lost nothing of its strength. In Prague, Rome and Paris, the progress of Hitlerism in Germany has added new force to the objections to a programme which would add seven millions of people to the Reich, bring German frontier posts to the Karawanken and the Brenner, and make of the Czechs a mere ethnic island in the Teutonic sea. The Austrian experiment has failed, but the reasons which explain it have lost nothing of their vitality. On the contrary, the announcement of the projected tariff union of March, 1931, was accepted in the capitals of the Status Quo powers as a threat to European peace, hardly less serious than the ultimatum to Serbia in July, 1914.

Chapter Nine

HUNGARIAN IRREDENTISM

BETWEEN the dominant races in the two halves of the old Hapsburg Monarchy, the resemblances were only political. Each ruled in a state in which it constituted a minority. But while the patriotism of the Austrian, such as it was, had an imperial character, that of the Hungarian was at once territorial and ethnic. More than a thousand years before the World War, this Asiatic tribe had crossed the Carpathians, ridden down into the Pannonian Plain, off-saddled and settled. Hitherto nomadic, the followers of Arpad became henceforth fixed upon the territory they had conquered, and to which they promptly gave strategic frontiers, that were still in existence when the Assassination of Serajevo precipitated the World War. Like the Poles, with whom the Magyars have had many historical associations, and for whom they preserve instinctive sympathies, the Hungarians founded their state at a cross-roads of Europe. In their westward thrust they had separated the Slavs of Bohemia from those to the south of the Drave and the Danube, and had similarly placed themselves between the Teutons pushing down the Danube Valley and the Turks, who presently pressed forward in the long sustained advance, which was ultimately halted only under the walls of Vienna.

Hungarian history is, therefore, one long tale of wars waged against the German and Turk, and of power exercised over the Slav. The defeat of Mohacs, which brought in its train long servitude to Turkish rulers, and the never ceasing resistance, depopulated many of the border areas. Thus, when the Turk had at last been expelled, the Hungarians were compelled to invite German colonists to Transylvania and the Banat, while Rumanian and Slav immigrants, fleeing from Turkish oppression, established themselves in the south and east.

For the Hungarians, however, the fundamental unity of their country has always been that associated with the Crown of St. Stephen which antedated the period of Teutonic, Slav and Latin infiltration. All Magyar rulers at their coronation brandished their swords to west and east, to north and south, symbolically re-affirming the indestructible solidarity of a kingdom which had become almost millennial before the creation of the modern German Empire.

Yet within this kingdom and disregarding the

Croats beyond the Drave, and the relatively few Italians of Fiume, the Magyars were barely a majority. Essentially a people of the plain, they had left to the Slovaks all the highlands to the Polish Border. In Transylvania and the Banat, the Rumanians possessed a decisive numerical advantage. Even north of the Danube, alike in Pancsova and the lower Bachka, the majority was Serbian. Political power, however, rested uniquely in Magyar hands. Nor did their own long struggle for racial independence teach them respect for the ethnic aspirations of other people.

Essentially a soldier people, they have always regarded their title to their kingdom as established by the sword. Even in the Twentieth Century, a certain feudal relation survived alike between their Magyar landlords, and the peasants of all races. But the Magyar magnate and peasant shared the same sense, not alone of ethnic unity, but of racial superiority, in the face of other tribes. All of historic Hungary from the Tatra to the Save, and from the Leitha to the lower Danube, was the land of the Magyars, and all of the inhabitants therein were bound to acknowledge Hungarian supremacy and, in the end, to subordinate their own language and rights to the larger rights of the ruling race.

This conception of Hungary, one and indivisible, accompanied by a total and well nigh unconscious disregard for the rights of minorities, endured to the very end of the World War, and even in the hour of complete disaster, the possibility of the dismemberment of the ancient Kingdom hardly dawned upon the Hungarian people. Nor can any sympathy with the wrongs and injustices, which they suffered at the hands of the makers of the peace treaties, serve to disguise the fact that they measurably brought these upon themselves. The attitude of the German toward the Pole, of the Austrian toward the Czech, found exact repetition in that of the Magyar toward the Rumanian, the Slovak and the Serb within his domains. Only the Germans constituted a privileged race, and were thus permitted to enjoy political equality with the Hungarians.

If, on the ethnic map, pre-war Hungary was a centre of red indicating the Magyars, and encircled by colors marking the predominance of other races in all the border districts, economically it was a unit so clearly set off by natural frontiers, so closely bound together by geographical and economic ties, as almost to justify the Magyar claim that its unity had been fashioned by the Divine Will itself. To the Danube, which divided it into somewhat unequal halves, all the rivers of the north and east found their way either directly or through the Tiza. The great central Plain, flat as the proverbial pan-

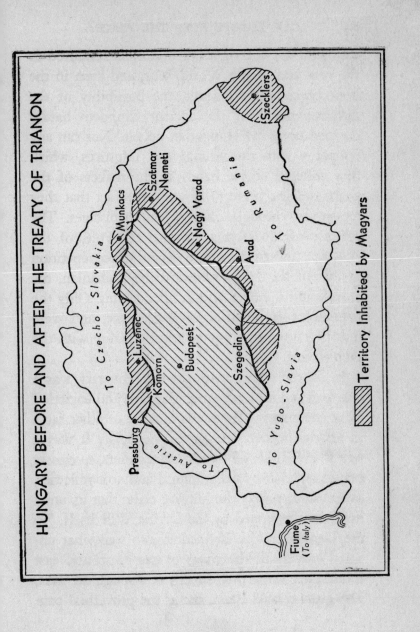

HUNGARY BEFORE AND AFTER THE TREATY OF TRIANON

To Czecho - Slovakia

Munkacs

Szatmar Nemeti

Nagy Varad

Szecklers

To Rumania

Arad

Luzenec

Budapest

Szegedin

Pressburg

Komorn

To Austria

To Yugo - Slavia

Fiume
(To Italy)

Territory Inhabited by Magyars

cake, occupied the heart of the country, which was itself inhabited by populations entirely Magyar, while the Slovaks of the north were separated from the Czechs by formidable mountain barriers, the Rumanians of Transylvania and the Banat, from those of the Regat, by the main wall of the Carpathians, and the Serbs of the Bachka, from those of Serbia, by the mighty Danube. On the southwest, too, the Drave was a natural frontier from Carinthia to its mouth.

To Budapest, all railways and highways ran, as those of Northern France, to Paris. Nature and ten centuries of custom had combined to make the Hungarian capital the economic, as well as the political centre, of this vast region. To undertake to divide this area into fractions determined by ethnic circumstances was economically as preposterous as to surround St. Louis and the immediately adjoining central states by political frontiers cutting the great transcontinental trunk lines.

And, since no natural barriers, no rivers or mountains marked racial limits, it involved drawing frontiers across the plains, shutting off the peoples of the hills from their markets in the cities of the plains, and exposing the peoples of the lowlands to floods coming from the mountains inhabited by populations unconcerned with river regulations. Nowhere else in a Central Europe, stricken by the folly of ethnic frontiers, is it possible to discover such defiance of all economic and commercial considerations as about Szeged, Szabodka, Nagy Varad and Losoncz.

Nevertheless, once the principle of self determination had been invoked, it was clear that the character of the border populations must determine the surrender by the Hungarians of Slovakia, the larger portion of the Banat and even a portion of the Bachka, along with Croatia. And once more, as in the borderlands of the Germans and Poles, the task of drawing equitable frontiers was complicated by an age-long intermingling of races. Moreover, precisely as the Germans of East Prussia constituted an ethnic island cut off from the Germans of the Reich by the projection of Slavic population, extending from the Netze to the Baltic, the Szecklers, in the Carpathians constituted a solid block of Magyars occupying three counties, but separated from the mass of their fellow-countrymen by a wide band of Rumanian population.

No boundary system was conceivable, therefore, which did not result, not merely in a far-reaching mutilation of the millennial kingdom, but also in the creation of very considerable Magyar minorities within the limits of the Succession States. To grievances which were inevitable, however, there were added injustices which were avoidable. Thus Hun-

gary was deprived, not alone of lands in which the alien majority was overwhelming, and others in which it was at least theoretical, but also on a wide circle on the whole northern frontier from Pressburg to Munkacs, and on the eastern, from Munkacs to the Danube, lands were taken containing almost a million and a half of Magyars, living in solid ethnic blocks adjoining the new Hungarian boundary. In fact, in dealing with the Magyars, the statesmen of Paris permitted their friends of the Succession States a license comparable only with that victorious generals in another age occasionally suffered their troops in a city taken by storm.

No frontier, of all the many traced at the Paris Peace Conference was at once as fantastic and as inequitable as that which between the Danube and the Upper Tiza cut off nearly three quarters of a million of Magyars from Hungary, and without ethnic or economic justification, transferred them to the new state of Czecho-Slovakia. Not less wanton were the mutilations incident to the satisfaction of the Rumanian demand to possess the strategic railway lines connecting Szatmar on the north, and Arad on the south, with Nagy Varad, which created still another Magyar minority, this time numbering half a million. Precisely the same considerations dictated the transfer to Serbia of Szbadka and its surrounding countryside with more than a quarter of millions of Magyars.

Szeged, the second city of Hungary, was almost enclosed in the net of Slav and Rumanian frontiers which separate purely Magyar populations, while the cession of the Island of Schutt to Czecho-Slovakia, despite the total absence of even a Slavic minority in its population, brought Budapest within range of Big Berthas which could be produced in the foundries of Skoda and mounted on Slovak territory. Moreover, in the case of Hungary, the Paris Conference did not, as in that of Germany, solve a problem presented by the collision between the equal rights of an enemy and a friendly state, to the profit of the latter. On the contrary, while more than three millions of Magyars were transferred to Slav and Rumanian rule, not ten per cent of this number of Slavs and Latins were left within Hungarian frontiers, and the relative proportions of the two minorities disclose the character of the division.

Thus the partition of Hungary at Paris was only measurably less complete than that of Poland at Vienna. That any nation could patiently accept such a settlement, or ever voluntarily resign itself to such mutilation, was obviously unthinkable. Least of all, however, was it conceivable for the Hungarian people, whose thousand years of history had been marked by uncompromising resistance to similar dismemberments. In the first emotion of despair, following the arrival of rumors of the contemplated partition, the Hungarian people surrendered to Bolshevism. That phase swiftly passed, but thereafter, to the present hour, the whole Hungarian people remain unreconciled and irreconcilable in the face of their present frontiers.

Hungarian irredentism thus confronts Europe with the demand for the revision of the Treaty of Trianon. It is true, too, that for many Magyars the demand extends to all of the territories which once constituted the Kingdom of St. Stephen. On the other hand, time has brought with it, even in Budapest, a perception of the impossibility of restoring the state which disappeared in 1919. Far more general today, is the demand for the immediate return of the lands in which the Hungarian majorities are undeniable, the protection of the racial rights of the minorities beyond these areas and, in a distant future, perhaps, the submission to the inhabitants of the Banat and Transylvania, as well as of Slovakia, of the question as to what allegiance they prefer. And until justice in the matter of the immediate demands is assured, Hungary remains intransigeant and morally insurgent.

Inevitably, however, Hungarian demand for Treaty revision awakens identical apprehensions in Prague, Bucharest and Belgrade. Naturally, too, this apprehension has led to military agreements and political alliances designed to perpetuate the status quo. Thus the Little Entente encircles Hungary with bayonets, and the Magyars, permanently disarmed by the Treaty of Trianon, have lived continuously in the fear of formidable armies always within less than a week's march of the capital, which has already known a Rumanian occupation.

Fear, hate and suspicion exist everywhere along these new frontiers, and oppression and persecution of the Magyar minorities, while it varies in form and degree, is discoverable in all of the Succession states. Economic coöperation, in the face of this political condition, is well-nigh impossible and, in point of fact, the material hardships of the populations in the districts forcibly torn from Hungary, has even exceeded that within the mutilated fragment that remains.

It is plain, however, that no treaty revision, even remotely satisfactory to the Hungarians, could fail to re-establish Slav and Latin minorities within the Magyar State or to deprive the Succession states of cities, railway lines and highways, which are of great economic or strategic importance. And even were Czech, Rumanian or Serb statesmen minded to make sacrifices in the effort to arrive at a durable settlement, their own publics would repudiate the agreements and destroy the authors. Thus, even Benes, who once advocated territorial sacrifices in return for permanent reconciliation, has renounced his own proposals and taken his stand with uncompromising Czech nationalism.

Chapter Ten

CZECHS AND THEIR MINORITIES

WOODROW WILSON was not alone the architect of
the Polish Corridor but, in addition, in no small degree responsible for the creation of the Czecho-
Slovak state. Thus the American traveller, who
descends from his train in the Wilson station at
Prague, or pauses before the Wilson monument in
Posen, is impressively reminded of events forgotten
in the United States but preserved in the memories
of two grateful peoples.

In the case of the Czechs, as of the Poles, Wilson's championship had far-reaching consequences
for Europe. For, as the restoration of the Polish
Corridor destroyed German unity, the creation of
an independent Bohemia insured the complete disintegration of the Hapsburg Monarchy. Once the
Czechs had withdrawn, all possibility was abolished of any form of political association between
the central portions of Austria-Hungary.

On the economic side, no decision of the Paris
Conference was as disastrous, since it broke asso-

ciations which had endured for centuries and separated regions which were interdependent. By contrast, on the political side, this dissolution of secular ties not only seemed inevitable at Paris, but had, in fact, already proceeded far, and perhaps irrevocably, before the Peace Conference assembled.

In reality, in the councils of the Allied and Associated Powers of 1919 the old Hapsburg Monarchy was without a friend or advocate. The reason was simple. For a full century Austria had been the symbol of oppression in Europe, and Vienna the centre of reaction on the Continent. The wrongs of racial minorities on both banks of the Leitha were notorious. And in the minds of all Allied peoples, the share of Austria in the responsibility for the World War itself, was still unforgettable.

Thus, for his resolution to create an independent Czech state, Wilson found not merely French, but also British support. Nevertheless, the difficulties in the pathway were not only patent, but formidable. Czech independence had expired in the Battle of the White Mountain three centuries before the final campaign of the World War. Even before the Thirty Years War, the Hussite struggles had resulted in the practical extermination of the Czech nobility. For generations the very sense of race and culture had been lost. Thus, while the liberation of Poland was no more than a restoration, the re-establishment of Czech independence amounted to a renaissance.

On the political side, the Czechs themselves had long hesitated over the question of seeking absolute independence. Thus, in the Nineteenth Century, when the re-awakening of racial consciousness occurred, Czech ambition was directed not at separation, but federation. In a word, this Slavic tribe sought to exercise the same measure of control within their own provinces of Bohemia, Moravia and Austrian Silesia that the Germans and Austrians exercised in their respective halves of the Dual Monarchy.

This aspiration, patently reasonable in itself, was, however, incompatible with Austrian interests, for obvious reasons. Within these provinces, which together contained a decisive Czech majority, dwelt an important German minority. And this minority, together with the Germans of Austria Proper, constituted the ruling race in the Northern half of the Dual Monarchy. Thus Czech ambitions came into square collision with the prerogatives of the race, which through long centuries had controlled the destinies of the centre of Europe.

In the face of this Czech challenge, the German 'Austrians had made a tacit alliance with their Polish subjects of Galicia, allowing them political control in this portion of the old Polish state in which there was no considerable German minority. Cracow had thus become the spiritual and cultural capital of a Poland which politically did not exist, and, in return, Polish deputies in the Austrian Parliament had voted with the German, and against the Czech. As a consequence of this division between the Slavs, Czech sympathies had always been Russian, and this pre-war hostility was accentuated after the close of the conflict, when Czech and Polish claims collided in Teschen.

At Paris, Allied statesmen were plainly influenced, in the case of the Czechs, by the example of Switzerland as they had been in that of Austria by the experience of Belgium. In the Helvetian Confederation, Germans, French and Italians had dwelt together almost immemorially, and the reality of the national unity of this Alpine republic was undeniable. To Wilson and his associates, therefore, it seemed not only possible, but even probable, that Czechs and Germans, living together in a territory with far more obvious natural frontiers, would repeat the achievement in racial adjustment of the three peoples of the Swiss Cantons.

Once more, as in the case of Austria, however, the effort to turn out a ready-made state upon the model of another, which owed its development to long centuries of evolution, proved unsuccessful. And the explanation lay in the totally different relation, which had for long existed between the Czechs and Germans of Bohemia, from that which through the centuries had endured between Latin and Teuton in Switzerland. For the Swiss races had always lived together as equals, while the status of German and Czech was that of superior and inferior. And during the war itself, while Austrian jails had been crowded with Czech prisoners, Austrian generals attributed many defeats to the desertion of Czech regiments on the field of battle.

Nevertheless, while the races were irreconcilable, the lands which they inhabited were indivisible. Both Czech and German peoples were equally agreed that all attempts to divide Bohemia and Moravia on ethnic lines could only produce utter economic disaster. Thus the actual basis of dispute between the two races does not arise from any question of boundary, but is, in fact, a far deeper issue, which involves the existence of the Czech state itself.

For the German minority, counting above a third of the population of Bohemia, Moravia and Austrian Silesia, which lives in a wide circle along the frontiers of Bavaria, Saxony and German Silesia, seeks union with Germany. But since such union would bring economic ruin, unless the Slavic regions were also joined to the Reich, it also dreams of a future in which the Czech nation will be sub-

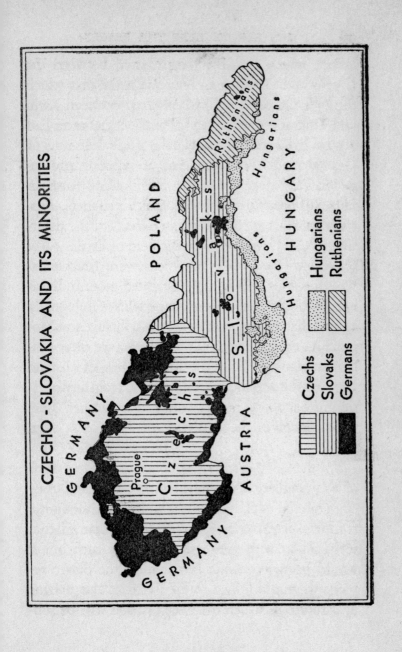

CZECHO-SLOVAKIA AND ITS MINORITIES

GERMANY

POLAND

Prague

Czechs

Slovaks

Ruthenians

Hungarians

Hungarians

GERMANY | AUSTRIA

HUNGARY

Czechs
Slovaks
Germans

Hungarians
Ruthenians

merged in a greater Germany as it was once in ancient Austria.

Toward such a goal, it is patent, the union of Austria itself with the Reich would constitute a long step. Then the Czech provinces would be no more than a Slavic Cape Cod projecting into a German ocean. Bohemia would become strategically the citadel of the German world. But remembering the old military maxim—"Who holds Bohemia, holds Germany" the Czechs are under no illusion as to the length of time they would be permitted to garrison the heart of the new Greater Germany. Nor are they less acutely aware that the Anschluss would mean for them an almost complete encirclement by German frontiers, and the transfer to German hands of practically every line of communication with the outside world.

Justly impressed by the hazardous situation of the Czechs, the statesmen of Paris took another momentous step, which was to join the Slovaks of the Carpathian highlands of Hungary to the new Bohemia. On the ethnic side this union was clearly justifiable for, although the differences between their dialects are considerable, both tribes are Slavic, and are more closely related to each other than to any of their neighbors. Historically, on the other hand, there was no tradition of association.

For centuries the Czechs had been bound to the House of Hapsburg, while for a thousand years the Slovaks had followed the fortunes of the Magyars.

Geographically, this union produced a state of absurd dimensions. The distance between Eger on the German frontier and the ultimate Ruthenian hamlet on the Rumanian border is greater than that between Paris and Berlin, but between the Polish and Hungarian frontiers, less than that from Paris to Rheims. This political union, too, was made in clear defiance of all physical circumstances, for all the rivers, valleys and natural lines of communication from the Slovak upland run south to the Hungarian Plain, while mountain ridges bar the way between Slovakia and Bohemia.

This union of the Czechs and Slovaks not only involved fresh and disastrous economic dislocations, but also inescapably produced further racial confusion. For, although the Slovaks constitute a majority in their province, the eastern third is inhabited by a solidly Ruthenian population, while the southern borderlands contain a considerable mass of Magyars. And if, at the moment, the Ruthenian minority discloses no passionate eagerness for union with its ethnic brethren who inhabit the Ukraine and Eastern Galicia, the Hungarians, on the contrary, look forward with undisguised determination to reunion with their fellow-Magyars beyond frontiers which have no racial warrant.

Czecho-Slovakia, as created by the Paris Peace Conference is then a land of minorities, a country in which, in fact, there is no majority. By one of the oddest and most ironical of necessities, the statesmen of Paris, who undertook to resolve the Hapsburg Monarchy into its ethnic fractions in accordance with the rights of peoples, found themselves in the end condemned to create a new state in which the racial elements were as diverse and as irreconcilable as in either the Austrian or Hungarian states of the pre-war era.

In this new state majority rule is achieved by the alliance of rather more than six millions of Czechs with materially less than three millions of Slovaks. But a German minority of considerably more than three millions sets its face toward Berlin, a Magyar minority of not far from a million looks to Budapest, and a Ruthenian minority of half a million will, beyond all question, one day look either to Moscow or to Kiev, if Ukrainian independence becomes a reality.

Again, the national aspirations of these six millions of Czechs constitute the single physical obstacle to the union of more than sixty-five millions of Germans of the Reich, seven millions of the Austrian Republic, and three of Czecho-Slovakia itself, to association in a Greater Germany, which has become the ideal of all. Thus the will of nearly eighty millions is in conflict with that of less than seven, and the Czechs are condemned to seek abroad, and in alliance, a security otherwise beyond attainment.

No people on the European Continent then, can be said to live as perilously or as precariously as the Czechs. Their existence is permanently endangered by the national and racial purposes of the great German people. Their territorial unity on the south is menaced by the immutable purpose of the Hungarians, whose numbers also exceed those not alone of the Czechs, but of Czechs and Slovaks combined. To have lived at all, to have, in addition, made a measure of political progress and attained a degree of economic prosperity, testifies to the unmistakable fact that the Czechs are the most capable of all the Slavic tribes. Nor is it less an evidence of the ability of Masaryk and Benes, that they have achieved for their country stability at home and an influence and position in European councils not equalled by nations whose population is far greater and whose circumstances are much less hazardous.

In the face of the geographical, political and racial circumstances of Czecho-Slovakia, however, the position of its people and its statesmen on the question of the revision of the treaties of Versailles, St.

Germain and Trianon, alike is unmistakable. For while revision means mutilation for Poland, it spells extinction for Czecho-Slovakia. And in such extinction, Anschluss would be the first and the decisive step.

Chapter Eleven

ADRIATIC AND BALKAN QUESTIONS

THE dissolution of the Hapsburg Monarchy raised still another territorial issue, and provoked a further quarrel between peoples. And this time the peoples at odds had been allies of the war. As the Poles and Czechs had disputed the possession of Teschen, the Italians and Southern Slavs came to grips over the whole eastern littoral of the Adriatic. Here, too, the opposing policies of status quo and revision were advocated not by the victors and vanquished of the war, but by peoples whose triumph or defeat was a detail of the Peace Conference itself.

In reality, both the Southern Slavs and Italians emerged from the Paris Conference equally dissatisfied with the result. By the secret treaties of the war period, Fiume had been assigned to the new union of the Slavic tribes, which had already been foreshadowed, while the northern half of Dalmatia was similarly earmarked for Italy. But, at Paris, Wilson had sought to obtain both Fiume, and all of Dalmatia, for the Slavs. His failure in the former case provoked Serbian resentment, while his success in the latter, aroused enduring Italian indignation.

When, after Paris, D'Annunzio made a theatrical descent upon Fiume and put Europe in the presence of still another accomplished fact, which was beyond the power of the Allied nations to modify, the relations between Italy and Yugo-Slavia entered upon a long period of tension, during which actual conflict frequently seemed unavoidable. Moreover, while a *modus vivendi* presently ensued, the passions awakened by the long crisis and the aspirations of the peoples at odds, made subsequent reconciliation impossible.

The question raised immediately over Fiume, but in fact extending to the whole shore of the Adriatic from the pre-war Italian frontier to the Albanian, recalls in its geographical details the dispute between the Poles and the Germans in the Baltic. As the German populations from Puck to the Pregel, even where they constitute a local majority, occupy territory which is no more than the façade to a vast hinterland, entirely inhabited by Poles, so from the mouth of the Isonzo to that of the Boyana, Italian majorities in Trieste, Pola, and in Fiume, itself, merely occupy the waterfront of a region extending from the coastal hills to the Drave, in which the population is purely Slavic.

On the economic side, to interpose political frontiers and customs barriers between this waterfront and the Slavic hinterland is as illogical as to hand over Boston, New York and Baltimore, with their immediate environs to Britain, while leaving all the back country in its present situation; Trieste and Fiume were alike, naturally, and as a consequence of their development, the ports of all the region which had once been under the sway of the Hapsburgs. And while Austria had favored one, Hungary had lavished money on the other. Expensive and admirable trunk railway lines led from the valleys of the Drave and Save to these ports. Trade and commerce flowed easily and in great volume by these routes. To cut these lines by new frontiers was to render the railways useless and to doom the ports to decline, and even to decay.

On the political side, the extension of the territory of the Southern Slavs to the Adriatic inevitably created another ethnic battleground. Historically, the association of this coastland was Latin. Nowhere, even along the shores of the Mediterranean itself, are the monuments of Roman occupation more splendid. And beside them—and even at times superimposed upon them—are many of the rarest achievements of Venetian builders. Thus as Spalato recalls Diocletian, Ragusa reflects the glory of the Doges. And today, as in all past centuries,

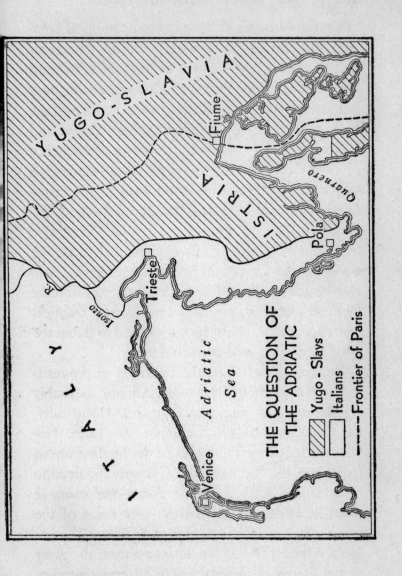

YUGO-SLAVIA

ISTRIA

Fiume

Quarnero

Pola

Trieste

Isonzo

ITALY

Adriatic Sea

Venice

THE QUESTION OF
THE ADRIATIC

Yugo - Slavs
Italians
Frontier of Paris

Trieste, Pola and Fiume, like Zara, significantly named *Italianissima*, contain Italian majorities.

By contrast, from Gorizia to Cattaro, the Italian population is but a Latin fringe to a solid Slavic mass, and even to give Trieste tangency to Italy, and to join Fiume to Istria, it was necessary to create a Slavic minority numbering more than three quarters of a million within the new frontiers of Italy. Thus, as before 1914, there had existed an Italian Irredenta in this corner of Europe; after 1919, there was substituted a region, viewed by the Southern Slavs, as an unredeemed fraction of their fatherland.

Bitterness between the two races was of long standing. Not only had the Hapsburgs sought to modify the character of the town of Trieste by encouraging the infiltration of Slovenians and Croats, but in the years when they had ruled in the valley of the Po, they had drawn their garrisons from their Slav populations. And the memory of oppression and tyranny sustained by the bayonets of Croatian and Slovenian garrisons has not yet vanished from Milan or Verona. Again, during the World War itself, it was the Slav troops of the Dual Monarchy which held the line of the Isonzo against Italy and inflicted frightful casualties, alike at the Carso, and on the Bainzizza Plateau.

All these traditional rancors were reanimated

when the two races came into collision at the Paris Peace Conference and the settlements eventually arrived at—some of them only after acts of violence—were equally unsatisfactory to both. For the Slavs, the enforced resignation of the ports, which were their natural gateways on the open sea, and the transfer of hundreds of thousands of their fellow Slavs to alien rule, which promptly proved oppressive, was not a solution of the problem, but only a temporary postponement of that adjustment which they were resolved to obtain.

For the Italians, on the other hand, the rise of the Southern Slav State was a complete and bitter disillusionment. With the downfall and disintegration of the Hapsburg Monarchy, they had hoped to achieve not merely the recovery of the Italian populations which after 1866 had still remained under Austrian rule, but also a position of power and influence in all the region of the Danube and the Drave. But instead, after the Paris Conference, they found themselves confronted by a young and vigorous state, whose King, whatever the other causes for dissension within his newly extended frontiers, could always re-unite his quarrelling tribes whenever an Italian question was raised.

This new Slav state, not only challenged the territorial unity of Italy, since it never concealed its purpose to acquire Trieste and Fiume, and similarly closed the way to Italian influence in Southeastern Europe, but also, by its association with France, brought Italy face to face with the unwelcome prospect of a war on two fronts. And as her eastern land frontiers are menaced by Southern Slav armies trained by French officers, and equipped by French factories, and supported by French loans, her mastery of the Adriatic is compromised by French-built submarines flying Yugo-Slav colors.

This direct clash between Italian and Southern Slav where their boundaries actually join, has led also to an indirect collision over the control of the Albanian state. Albania, itself, had gained national independence as a result of the joint efforts of Austria and Italy to prevent Serbian access to the sea during the Balkan Wars of 1912-13. Greece and Serbia had agreed to divide Albania between themselves, in advance of their attack upon Turkey in 1912, the line of division to be the Skumbi River.

After long delays, during which the presence of Serbian troops at Durazzo, and the siege of Skutari by the Montenegrins, nearly precipitated a general European conflict, since Russia championed the cause of the Serbs, the will of a United Europe, functioning for the last time, fashioned an Albanian state. But the frontiers of this new state, which was totally incapable of defending itself, were equally inacceptable to the Greeks in the south, and the Serbs in the north. Moreover, Europe, having erected Albania, and raised a score of flags on a ruined palace in Skutari as witness of the international protection resting over the principality, promptly plunged into the universal tumult of the World War.

During the struggle Albania was a battlefield; after the war Italy reserved for herself, with the assent of her allies, a privileged position in the restored principality. But the Albanians themselves, a people who antedate all but the Basques in European occupation, soon forced the Italian garrisons at Valona to depart. Italian policy then shifted, and with the coming of the Fascists, Mussolini adopted the rôle of a protector, rather than a master. This rôle was equally obnoxious to Greek and Slav, and the killing of an Italian officer on the Greek frontier provoked the Duce to the descent upon Corfu, which did little credit to his wisdom as a statesman, and less honor to Italian arms.

By virtue of this Italian policy, however, Tirana, the Albanian capital became a centre of intrigue and the battleground of Italian and Southern Slav influences. Thus less than a decade after the whole European Continent had been devastated by a general war precipitated by the assassination of Serajevo, its peace was again placed at the mercy of a tavern brawl in Tirana, or a quarrel between Slav and Italian sailors at Durazzo. For, as the old Serbia had been the ward of Russia, the new Yugo-Slavia was the ally of France against Italy, and of Czecho-Slovakia and Rumania, against Hungary. Concomitantly, Italian diplomacy sought to exploit Magyar resentment due to Serbian possession in the Bachka and Bulgarian passion born of Serbian rule in Macedonia.

This question of Macedonia and of the Treaty of Neuilly, which gave it the form in which it today disturbs the tranquillity of Europe, is for the Bulgarians what that of the Corridor is for the Germans, and that of their many lost provinces for the Magyars. Between 1912 and 1918 the Bulgarians fought the Turk, the Greek and Serbian, and finally in the World War, took up arms against the Allies, to possess this rugged and forbidding region which is today partitioned between the Greeks and Serbians.

Historically, the region has been held alike by Greeks, Bulgarians and Serbians. It was the seat of Alexander the Great. Ochrida was the capital of the Bulgarian Czar, Simeon; and Salonica, as well as Monastir, belonged to the shortlived empire of Stephen Dushan. Racially the population so far as it is neither Greek nor Turkish is of unmistakably mixed origin, but just as clearly the majority holds itself to be Bulgarian, and in 1919, as after the first

Balkan War seven years before, would have chosen union with its eastern, rather than its northern, neighbor.

Small as is its area and population relatively, too, it has played a great role in the history of contemporary Bulgaria, because it was the centre of the movement of national awakening. It has supplied that state with its political leaders as well as its teachers and, although never, save during the years of the World War after the conquest of Serbia, actually in Bulgarian hands, has exercised a decisive influence upon Bulgarian politics. Even today, although dominated by Serbian military forces, it is still a region of unrest, and neither the majority of the inhabitants, nor the people of Bulgaria, itself, are reconciled to the status quo.

Like the Magyars, however, the Bulgarian people have suffered mutilation on many sides. The Silistrian strip taken by Rumania in 1913 was not restored at Paris, while Bulgaria's outlet on the Aegean, cut in half when Greece acquired Kavalla after the Second Balkan War, was totally abolished by the Treaty of Neuilly, which established Hellenic rule from the west bank of the Maritza to the old frontiers of the Treaty of Bucharest. Three wars, infinite sacrifice and incredible suffering have, then, left Bulgaria the smallest of the old Balkan states. But these successive disasters have

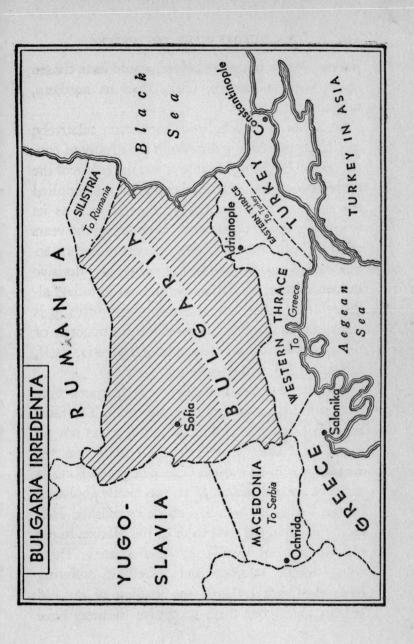

BULGARIA IRREDENTA

RUMANIA

YUGO-
SLAVIA

BULGARIA

SILISTRIA
To Rumania

• Sofia

MACEDONIA
To Serbia

• Ochrida

GREECE

Salonika•

Aegean
Sea

WESTERN THRACE
To Greece

EASTERN THRACE
To Turkey

Adrianople •

TURKEY

Constantinople •

Black
Sea

TURKEY IN ASIA

not broken the spirit of the people, nor modified their resolution to recover their lost lands, of which Macedonia is both materially and morally the most considerable in their eyes.

Like Berlin, Vienna, and Budapest, Sofia is, then, the capital of a people who are unreconciled to their present fate, and the Bulgarian people, like the German, Austrian and Magyar, are united in the determination to achieve a revision of the Paris Settlement. Watched by Greek, Serb and Rumanian armies, and themselves forcibly disarmed and forbidden to maintain forces sufficient even to defend their national territory, they still dream of the recovery of Monastir and Kavalla and, although temporarily helpless, refuse to accept as definitive, conditions which are beyond their present power to modify.

And this refusal is a permanent challenge alike to Serb, Greek and Rumanian security. For Bulgarian possession of Macedonia would cut the road of the Yugo-Slavs to the Aegean; Bulgarian recovery of Thrace would deprive Greece of a territory now thoroughly Hellenized as a consequence of the settlement of the Greek emigrants from Asia Minor, and finally, Bulgarian return to Silistria, would constitute a perpetual threat to the Rumanian line of communication which leads from Bucharest to Constanza. Here, as elsewhere, it is the vital interests of peoples which are in shock, and compromise is equally inconsistent with all national resolutions. Thus, while Central Europe has been Balkanized, the original Balkans remain unchanged.

Chapter Twelve

CHARACTER OF THE ISSUES

EXAMINATION of the territorial issues must, then, lead to two inescapable conclusions. For the peoples at odds, these issues are questions which involve national liberty, unity or security, in a word, precisely those things which peoples, ever since they came to power in nations, have been prepared to fight to defend and ready to die to acquire. And, again, in these issues, the rights of the contesting peoples are irreconcilable, for by reason of the physical, ethnic and economic circumstances, recognition of the rights of one nation must be at the sacrifice of those of another.

Thus, in the case of the Polish Corridor, it is literally true that there can be only a German or a Polish solution. There is no middle ground. It is German unity against Polish. It is German territorial contact with East Prussia or Polish outlet to the sea. But above and beyond all else, it is the question of the German and Polish inhabitants of the whole region of the Lower Vistula. And for the

American people, who fought a great civil war to preserve national unity, the purpose and will of both the Teutonic and the Slavic peoples should be utterly comprehensible.

Anschluss would result in the creation of a Germany, greater in area and population than the Hohenzollern Empire of 1914. It would instantly threaten the independence and, in fact, the existence of the Czech state as it would significantly restore the conditions which three centuries ago led to the extinction of the independence of this little Slavic tribe. For Poland, this reënforcement in power would strengthen a Germany resolved to suppress the Corridor, and recover Upper Silesia.

For France, the union of Austria and Germany would swell to more than seventy millions the population of a state whose numbers now vastly exceed the forty millions of the French Republic. It would restore the Mitteleuropa of the war, to abolish which, was one of the major war aims of France from 1914 to 1918. It would reincarnate that Holy Roman Empire against which, under Hapsburg sway, the House of Bourbon struggled from the age of Henri IV to the eve of the French Revolution. It would, in sum, place the hegemony of Europe within German reach, and thus reduce France, for all future time, to the condition and servitude of a second class power.

For Italy, the Anschluss would bring even more immediate perils. The frontiers of the greater Germany would join Italian, in regions where a German minority still cries out against Italian annexation. But these regions of the Southern Tyrol constitute the strategic key to the Italian Plain, the accustomed pathway of Teutonic invasion in the centuries extending backward to the age of the Hohenstauffens. In the same way, the arrival of the Reich at Klagenfurt and Villach would constitute an instant challenge to Italian possession at Trieste, the old port of the Hapsburg Monarchy on the sea, which in all Pan-German propaganda is predestined to serve as the Hamburg of the Adriatic.

For Czecho-Slovakia, the Anschluss constitutes a threat to its independence; for Poland, a danger to its unity; to France and Italy, the destruction of security. By contrast, the people of Austria are German; their right to decide their own political association is inherent in the democratic doctrine of self-determination. And their present economic condition is one of utter and apparently irremediable misery. Thus the collision of rights is again unmistakable.

And once more the American parallels hold good. On the one hand, the whole conception of American security has for a century been based upon that Monroe Doctrine, which asserts the right of the American people to exclude European peoples from effecting any new lodgment of South American shores or elsewhere in the two Americas. And, at the close of the Civil War, the readiness of the United States to fight to enforce this essentially status quo doctrine, dictated the withdrawal of French troops from Mexico. But, on the other hand, the course pursued by the United States, in the matter of Texas, is precisely that which the German would adopt in respect of Austria. Thus, in their own practice, the American people must discover precedent for the policies of both groups of nations at odds over the Anschluss.

For the Czech, Rumanian and Southern Slav peoples, revision of the Treaty of Trianon to satisfy the most moderate of the demands of Hungarian irredentism would require sacrifices, which illustrated in American circumstances would mean the surrender of whole states and the transfer of millions of people to other countries. The Hungarian frontier would be brought back to the site from which Belgrade was bombarded in 1914. The lines of communication between the Czech and Slovak halves of the new Slavic republic, vital alike for commercial and strategic considerations, would pass again into Magyar hands. Rumania would be called upon to cede a territory greater in area and population than Alsace-Lorraine, and having a

larger Latin population than existed in the Reichsland in 1871. But can any American conceive of a
president, a political party, a national Congress as-
senting to similar sacrifices?

Standing on the banks of the Vistula, the Danube
or the Maros, the American traveller has only to
examine the meaning in fact of all the various proposals for the revision of the territorial decisions
of the Paris treaties, has merely to translate these
proposals into terms of his own national geog-
raphy, to understand why resistance to them is
unanimous in the nations whose frontiers they menace. But in Berlin, Vienna or Budapest, the same
traveller cannot fail to conclude that had the United
States been dealt with after war as were Germany,
Austria and Hungary, peace without restitution
would be unthinkable for a hundred and twenty-
five million citizens of the American Republic, or
such fraction of these as still remained free.

Faced with the reality, having translated it into
the terms of the American national unity, such a
traveller would perceive at last how unfounded is
the familiar legend that these European territorial
disputes are the product of insensate nationalism
and unrestrained imperialism. He would be made
aware of the fact that in all these countries the
proportion of reasonable and peace-loving peoples
is not only the same, but identical with that in his

own. But he would also be brought inescapably to the conclusion that the gulf between these reasonable majorities in the several nations at odds is, to-day, impassable.

Exactly in the same fashion, the student who examined these territorial issues not on the ground, but in the light of history, would presently discover that the projects of treaty revision in the majority of cases simply envisage the substitution of an old system of force for the new, of ancient minorities for those of the present hour. He would see that the programme of the several Cabinets of republican Germany, in respect of the Polish Corridor, is no more than the old plan of partition of Frederick the Great, thinly disguised by the trappings of the doctrine of self-determination. Nor could he escape the ultimate conclusion that, if the collective power of three mighty empires had not been sufficient to extinguish the Polish will for national life and unity, a new partition modelled on the old would not provide a peace of understanding.

There is, too, another circumstance inescapable in Eastern and Central Europe, unrecognized in America and Britain. For both Anglo-Saxon peoples, the World War was utter folly, if not actual crime. In their eyes it resulted in human misery and material destruction unparalleled in history and unredeemed by any result. When, however, one passes German, Austrian or Hungarian frontiers, it is to enter countries for whose inhabitants the great conflict brought liberty and unity, and in whose eyes the World War holds the same place as the American Revolution in those of the people of the United States. And while the American Revolution resulted in the freeing of no more than three millions of colonists from a rule of their own race, the World War enfranchised more than forty millions, who lived under an alien tyranny and a foreign oppression which find no parallel in the experience of the people of the Thirteen Colonies.

Thus, the great convulsion, which, under western eyes, seems complete and unrelieved waste, takes on an utterly different aspect, when viewed from Warsaw, Prague, Belgrade or Bucharest, or in the capitals of the several Baltic states. In all these cities, knowledge of the horror and destruction of the conflict is measured by personal suffering and cost, but the tragedy, which goes beyond British or American experience, is redeemed by an independence, which constitutes a reward not disproportionate to any cost. And the people of the United States, who still erect their monuments to the honor of the authors of American independence and to the glory of the struggle which made that independence possible, can hardly refuse to recognize their own spirit in other races.

Again, the memory of an oppression still recent, makes the proposal for treaty revision, which for millions means the return to the old circumstances of tyranny, a threat of war, not a promise of peace. Less than two decades ago the Cossacks still patrolled the streets of Warsaw, and it is not yet fifteen years since the German army of occupation withdrew. The men who died for Czech independence in Austrian prisons are still within the living memory of many of their fellow countrymen. And the peoples who recall the sufferings which belong to their own lifetime, are similarly aware of the steps by which, in the long past, their independence was destroyed, and the circumstances under which their servitude began. We in the west have grown accustomed to liberty, but the peoples of the east of Europe have not yet had time to forget their chains, and for them revision of the territorial provisions of the peace treaties means a return to their prisons.

But, on the other hand, what western traveller, to whom the Germans of the Corridor, the Hungarians of Pressburg, Losoncz or Nagy Varad, the Austrians of South Tyrol, have even in the smallest measure, and despite the ever watchful eyes of their new masters, opened their tale of misery, of humiliation, of oppression, can fail to be moved deeply or to comprehend why life on present terms is intolerable, and to understand why the sufferings of these minorities awaken deep and enduring resolution in the hearts of the majorities of the same race who are still free, but today disarmed, and held to ransom.

Nothing is easier than to be roused to passionate indignation, either by the tales of ancient suffering, or of present misery. American and British travellers easily become the eager champions of one people or the enthusiastic advocates of another. But, in the end, all such emotions are equally futile. Viewed objectively the rights and wrongs take on the same aspect. The tragic reality is that these rights, equally appealing, these wrongs, similarly impressive, can lead only to war. For they are authentic rights and wrongs, and are, therefore, beyond the remedy of solutions based upon abstract principles and academic formulas. In a word, the territorial issues themselves, are insoluble in the light of the present spirit of ethnic nationalism.

PART THREE

NATIONAL POLICIES

Chapter   Thirteen

BASES OF POLICY

IT IS self evident that national policies in Europe must have their foundations, either directly or indirectly, in territorial issues. Outwardly these policies differ, as the conditions and interests of peoples are various. But although across national frontiers they take on monstrous proportions and are explicable only in terms of political folly and of moral obliquity, viewed objectively, they must seem in all American eyes hardly distinguishable.

Unfortunately American understanding of the policies of European nations is hampered by an unconscious adoption of the point of view of one of the various peoples actually in controversy. Instinctive, hereditary or accidental sympathies lead to ardent championship or violent condemnation. And in the post-war years an enormous European propaganda carried on in the United States with the obvious purpose of enlisting American support for each of the many national causes has further obscured the facts. Yet every European people's judgment of the policy of another is equally unreliable as a basis for accurate appraisal.

Thus the British, who view it as an example of unparalleled unselfishness that they should defend the liberty of Belgium, see in the same policy of France, in respect to Poland, only fresh proof of the traditional French ambition for European hegemony. As for the Germans, to them British solicitude for the rights of the Belgians, and French, for those of the Poles, appear a similar concern for national security covered by an identical pretense of regard for the sacredness of treaties.

Again, the French, who for half a century rejected all German proposals for reconciliation on the basis of the status quo and uncompromisingly demanded the return of Alsace and Lorraine as an antecedent condition to friendship, see in the German purpose to recover West Prussia and Silesia, proof of a willingness wantonly to destroy the peace of Europe. Nor do the Germans, who reckon French policy in respect of the Reichsland before 1914, one of the major causes of the World War, discover any spirit of *revanche* in their own purpose. Yet, for the rest of mankind, the distinction between the French attitude toward the Treaty of Frankfort and the German toward that of Versailles, is imaginary.

As for the people of the United States, since for

them security has always seemed conditioned upon isolation, their national policy has been continuously expressed in the prohibition of Europe lodgment upon American shores. But while, in the eyes of the people of the United States, this policy has taken on the appearance of a pure and disinterested championship of the liberties of the Latin Republics, for the peoples of these republics it is at once a threat of hegemony and in the light of Mexican history, a monument of hypocrisy. And for Europeans, the Monroe Doctrine is the frank and unvarnished expression of American imperialism.

In the same fashion, peoples who find the policies of their neighbors injurious to their own interests, or fatal to their conceptions of world order, not only pronounce the obnoxious doctrines immoral, but invariably charge them to the unregenerate and unrepresentative leadership which they discover easily in the offending nation. And they are always awaiting confidently a change in the domestic political situation which will produce a change in foreign policy.

Yet, while political control shifts frequently in every country, and new leaders appear regularly, national policies endure, little modified from generation to generation, and, indeed, from century to century. Labor Governments in Britain have shown themselves no less insistent upon the two power

naval standard in Europe, than their Tory predecessors. The programme of the German Republic,
in the matter of the Polish Corridor, is that of Frederick the Great. French policy, in respect of the
dominant state beyond the Rhine, has altered little
in the hands of Delcassé and Poincaré from the
form which it received at the hands of Richelieu
and Mazarin.

Precisely as peoples misunderstand the policies
of their neighbors, they also misinterpret the means
by which these policies are made effective. Thus an
island people, for whom the possession of a supreme fleet is the guarantee against invasion coming across the seas, identify the desire of a continental power for a supreme army to watch an open
frontier, as flagrant militarism. To the Italian, however, British naval supremacy in the Mediterranean,
and French military mastery of the Continent, appear similar expressions of an identical imperialism.

The same criticism extends to the political means
employed to sustain national policies. Thus the British, who, over and over again in their history have
organized coalition wars to check or break the
power of a continental state, find it inexplicable
that in peace a continental state should indulge in
military alliances. Nevertheless, it is equally patent
that the British have only abandoned their coalitions when the results of war have assured the in-

terests they took up arms to protect, and that the
military alliances of the Continent in peace time
are but the evidences of the persistence of perils
arising from the unsettled issues of conflict. As for
the German, who having been recently beaten by a
British coalition in war, now in peace finds himself
menaced by a French, he will hardly discover any
fine moral distinction between the two.

In sum, in the eyes of all peoples, the policies of
other nations seem based solely upon selfish considerations, while their own appear firmly established
on right and reason. But, in fact, all national policies are similarly founded upon purely parochial estimates of domestic interests and foreign dangers.
And, in support of these policies, every people em-
ploys the means it deems most appropriate, displays
the same unconcern for the effect of its policy upon
other nations, and rejects with utter scorn proposals
for amendment coming from abroad. Similarly, all
peoples found their programme of peace upon
changes of policy by other states, and their disarmament plans upon the renunciation of weapons useless in their own hands, but dangerous in those of
others.

It is, therefore, a pure waste of time to consider
national policies save in the eyes of the peoples,
who pursue them, and whose will and judgment
they express. To assume that collisions of national

policies constitute struggles between right and wrong, idealism and selfishness, democracy and reaction, in fact, between good and guilty peoples, is to end in a hopeless *impasse*. For while most countries have adopted the gold standard in respect of money, in the matter of policies they have retained their own currency, and none is redeemable at face value beyond domestic frontiers.

No illusion is, too, more common and more dangerous than that which assumes the existence of a world opinion, which will sweep away the barriers to international coöperation discoverable in the policies of individual countries. In the post-war period, such assumptions have invariably proven unfounded. It was as the self-appointed spokesman of this imaginary world opinion that Woodrow Wilson appealed to Italy in the matter of Fiume during the Paris Conference. But the unanimous voice of the Italian nation reinforced the demands of Orlando and Sonnino, which had provoked the Wilsonian appeal. Hoover had a similar experience with his Moratorium.

Confident that he voiced the sentiments of all other peoples, Charles E. Hughes went to New Haven and addressed a solemn protest to the French Nation against an occupation of the Ruhr. But Poincaré was not delayed for a single day by the protest, and French public opinion obeyed not international, but national inspiration. And, in precisely the same fashion, the utter unanimity of European public opinion on the subject of debt cancellation has served to anger, not to convert, the American people.

Half a generation after the event, the mass of the German people still reject the moral verdict passed by most of the rest of mankind upon the invasion of Belgium. Conceding the stupidities and follies which surrounded the action and for which their statesmen were responsible, the great majority of Germans still believe that their country, faced with utter ruin, was warranted in seeking escape from impending catastrophe by the Belgian route. Criticism of Bethmann-Hollweg for publicly describing the Treaty which guaranteed Belgian neutrality as a "scrap of paper" is unanimous, but condemnation of the Chancellor for thinking of it, as such, is rare.

The whole Wilsonian Adventure in Peace at Paris was based upon the conviction that, while European statesmen still remained subject to Old World ideas and principles which were narrowly nationalistic, the masses were dominated by a new international idealism. Thus the American President was satisfied that he had only to appeal to the peoples, over the heads of their prime ministers, to obtain a peace of justice and understanding. But to all peoples, beginning with the American, the Wilsonian appeals were without avail when they placed international idealism above national realism.

It is, then, with the clear perception that world opinion does not today go beyond the limits of what the several peoples believe all other nations ought to think, that the examination of the national policies of European states must be examined. For, in the post-war period, while the defeated nations have from time to time been constrained by force to modify their policies, temporarily, no people has yet consented to the voluntary abridgment of national purpose in the cause of international peace.

Chapter Fourteen

GERMANY

No TASK could conceivably be more difficult than that of presenting a clear and intelligible picture of German policy in the post war years. Not that the purpose of the German people has been obscure; on the contrary, with utter consistency and constancy, they have sought escape from the system of the Treaty of Versailles through abolition of reparations payments, removal of the unilateral disarmament circumstances and, finally, through revision of the territorial clauses of the treaty, as these fix the eastern frontiers of the Reich, and forbid union with Austria.

Clarity of purpose has, however, been accompanied by confusion in thought, which has resulted in disasters almost as complete as those of the war itself. Always, too, the German people have suffered from precisely the same psychological defects which explain the eventual arrival of nearly thirty nations in the ranks of their enemies during the World War. Convinced of the moral injustice

and the physical impossibility of the Paris Settlement, they have failed at all times to perceive the
cruel restrictions which hedge about a beaten people and limit the activities of a nation at once
disarmed and impoverished. Thus, in all German
effort there has been an absence of any sense of
measure and a fatal neglect of every reality.

Equally serious has been the handicap arising
from the absence of statesmen capable alike of defending German rights abroad, and of organizing
order at home. At Versailles the defeated Germany was able to send no diplomat like Talleyrand
to urge a case not different fundamentally from
that of France at Vienna, a century before. In domestic politics there were lacking a Thiers and a
Gambetta to restore order, re-establish government,
and vindicate authority. Thus ineptitude abroad
was accompanied by incoherence at home.

Responsibility for the lack of able foreign ministers alike before, during and after the World War
must, in the end, be laid at the door of Bismarck
himself. The Iron Chancellor had gathered into his
capable hands all the control and direction of the
Empire, which was his own handiwork. While he
reigned in Wilhelmstrasse, German policy was clear
and German prestige abroad unequalled. At the
Congress of Berlin, he proved himself the successor

of Metternich as the "coachman of Europe." But he brooked no equal, and trained no successor.

As a consequence, when William II dropped the old pilot and, undertook, himself, to direct the foreign policy of a great empire, he was unable to find competent ministers, as he was personally incapable of guiding the foreign affairs of his country. In Buelow he found a talented but dangerous servant, whose game of prestige awakened the apprehension of the Continent. And when Buelow fell, the court which had become Byzantine and the ministers, who were totally incompetent, blindly followed pathways which led, not by design, but by fatal ineptitude, to the supreme disaster.

When defeat came and the Emperor fled, the German people rather endured than shared in the revolution of November, 1918. What took place was not a popular rising like that in Paris in 1830, 1848, or 1870. A passive and almost voluntary bankruptcy removed an old régime, but in the republic which succeeded, all the traditional German particularism, which over long centuries had kept the German people divided and weak, reappeared. Then, and thereafter, there was lacking that instinct for self preservation, which always in times of crisis leads the French people to governments of public safety, and enables them to throw up a Gambetta, a Clemenceau or a Poincaré to meet perils, whether political, military or financial.

The constitution, which the German peoples adopted at Weimar, was a model of democratic theory, but for a people utterly untrained in the practice of self government, and totally incapable of domestic solidarity in the presence of perils at home or abroad, it was predestined to produce that incoherence and paralysis which have prevailed from 1919 to the present hour. Proportional representation forbade majority rule, and the particularism of the innumerable parties made administration a problem in tight rope walking, not a question of orderly government. And no comprehension of post-war Germany is possible which does not count with these two circumstances, the absence of leadership, and the impossibility of domestic political solidarity.

The terms of the Treaty of Versailles came to the German people as an utterly incomprehensible decision. In the pronouncements of Woodrow Wilson they had seen the promise of a generous peace and a prompt restoration of the German nation to its pre-war position. And, as a consequence, the complicated and terrible conditions of the Paris Settlement seemed at one time a violation of the Armistice terms on which surrender had been based and the revelation of a purpose to make German recovery impossible for all time. The moral, territorial, financial and military clauses of the treaty instantly took on, in all German eyes, an equal importance as details in a coherent programme, which was designed to keep a great people forever weak, impoverished and subject.

As a consequence, the German will to resist was immediate and unanimous. It was directed not against one portion of the treaty, but all. It expressed the instinct to live in the presence of a sentence of death. But unhappily for the German people, while, at least in its financial clauses, the treaty outran all possibility of fulfilment, and in its "guilt clause" passed human endurance, the power which was now in the hands of the victors who were to apply it, was absolute.

And in the tragic situation in which they found themselves, the Germans were not only without leadership, but they were also incapable of agreeing upon a course to pursue. Survivors of the old order urged a military alliance with Soviet Russia, satisfied that the spectre of this "Eastern Orientation" would terrify the victors of the war for whom it would assume the proportions of a forecast of a Bolshevized Europe.

Against this prescription of utter folly, other voices were raised in support of a policy of passive resistance, accompanied by partial fulfilment, until such time as the unreasonableness of the reparations programme was disclosed, and wisdom and judgment returned to victors, now intoxicated by the extent of their victory and, at the same time, appalled by the costs of their triumph.

But while partial fulfilment provoked the assassination of Erzberger and Rathenau, passive resistance, which extended to the military clauses, silenced British voices raised on behalf of the defeated enemy, while default in payments placed in French hands legal warrant for coercion. And concomitantly, the ostentatious flirtation with Moscow awakened an apprehension which insured the resort to force. Thus, close upon the heels of the Treaty of Rapallo, made by the Germans and Russians during the Conference of Genoa, with fatal consequences to that gathering, French troops marched into the Ruhr, and took the industrial life of Germany by the throat.

The result was never in doubt, and in September, 1923, nine months after the occupation of the Ruhr, Germany surrendered unconditionally. The first attack upon the Treaty of Versailles had failed, but the Ruhr War had been in many ways more disastrous than the World War itself. For while in the great conflict it had been the old, ruling class in Germany which had been overthrown, in the later campaign the middle class was destroyed, and the liquid capital of the Reich exhausted. Thus, at one time the foundations of domestic order were sapped, and Germany was condemned to seek abroad those funds necessary to operate her vast industrial machine.

After the Ruhr, Stresemann arrived. In him, Germany found, not alone the single competent domestic politician of the post war period, but also the sole successor of Bismarck in the foreign field. With equal courage and vision, he abandoned the "Eastern Orientation" and the policy of passive resistance. Like Thiers and Gambetta in 1871, he saw that the immediate problem was to restore the independence of his country by obtaining the evacuation of national soil, the abolition of financial control and return of Germany to the councils of Europe on the footing of a great power.

With absolute clarity he perceived that none of these things was possible save with the consent of the victors of the war, and in practice, this meant with the consent of France. This he purchased by the Truce of Locarno. The price Stresemann had to pay was set forth in the pacts of 1925. In the west, Germany recognized voluntarily that the status quo of Versailles was definitive. In the east, the Reich pledged itself to undertake no revision of frontiers by force. Thus the question of Alsace-Lorraine was removed from the list of European problems, and France, further fortified by British and Italian guarantees of the Locarnian contract in its Rhine detail, obtained a new assurance of security.

Nor is it less clear that the German people, themselves, were in the main prepared to resign their claims to Metz and Strasbourg in return for the recovery of their independence, and in the prospect of an early revision of the reparations and military clauses of the Treaty of Versailles. For the rest, no one more clearly than Gustav Stresemann, who had been a frank annexationist in the more prosperous days of the World War, before disaster came, envisaged the eventual recovery of the Corridor and the inevitable realization of the Anschluss. But like Gambetta, his counsel to his fellow-countrymen was never to forget, and never to mention the "lost provinces" of the eastern marches.

Locarno gave Germany substantially five years of relative calm, and in that time French troops left the Rhine, international commissions, financial and military alike, quit Berlin; the Dawes Plan, which had been the prelude to Locarno, was followed by the Young Plan, bringing further reductions in reparations. But even more important than all else, Germany at Geneva appeared once more in the guise of a great power, and Stresemann, together with Briand and Chamberlain, constituted a tri-

umvirate of peace and were literally masters of
Europe.

The death of Stresemann, however, marked the
end of the Truce of Locarno. That domestic political incoherence, to restrain which actually cost
Stresemann his life, promptly reappeared. Moreover, in the five years following the agreement of
Locarno, profound changes had taken place within
the Reich itself. Economically and psychologically,
Germany had begun to escape from the consequences of a lost war. The immediate post-war fear,
that the Reich was doomed to die, disappeared.
Something of the old confidence returned, memories of the great rôle the nation had played between 1870 and 1914 revived.

A new generation was, too, beginning to appear
on the stage. This generation had not known the
war. The horrors of the trenches, the agony of gas
warfare, the unimaginable miseries of conflict, alike
at the front and at home, were unknown to this
youth. On the contrary, it was confronted by a
national life restricted to limits within which opportunity was lacking. Responsibility for the disasters which had produced this reduction in national
stature, rested with another generation and a different régime, and the new Germany was equally
impatient of burdens inherited from the past and
restraints which dominated its present.

The departure of the French armies of occupation, and the disappearance of all representatives of international control, stimulated this sense of national strength and independence, but at the same time, intensified the resentment of handicaps still remaining. And these handicaps were twofold, the reparations payments, which continued, and the eastern frontiers, which had now endured for a full decade. Moreover, the original German conviction that Poland would collapse of its own incoherence was vanishing in the presence of a Polish Republic, visibly gaining not losing in stability.

German youth was, too, profoundly moved by the evidences which multiplied, not only of the rapid disappearance of German minorities within the lost provinces, but also of the ever mounting menace to the German populations alike in Danzig and East Prussia. But a disarmed and tribute-paying Germany was helpless, and thus the financial and disarmament clauses of the Treaty of Versailles took on in German eyes the character of a system designed to perpetuate the mutilation of the Reich, and to prepare the way for the loss of all German foundations at and beyond the Vistula.

Manifestly the German giant was again beginning to stir uneasily. And the evidences of this returning strength and developing purpose awakened apprehension in Paris, and natural fears in

Warsaw and Prague. These fears were stimulated by recurring demonstrations of war veterans on both the eastern and western frontiers. German nationalism roused French, which had viewed with profound disapproval and utter lack of faith, the evolution of French policy under the guidance of Briand, and in conformity with the spirit of Locarno, and although the great majority of the French people sincerely desired reconciliation and coöperation with Germany, their hope was new born while their fears were secular.

Then, finally, fell the great economic depression of 1930-1931. To the Germans the promised relief of the Young Plan proved illusory. Unemployment mounted into the millions, misery spread. The masses, who had recovered a measure of confidence after the terrible nightmare of the inflation period, suddenly found themselves reduced to circumstances which recalled recent suffering. The old régime, which had been dispossessed, the middle class, which had been impoverished, the youth, which saw the door of opportunity now doublebolted, shared the same feelings of despair. The illusion of Locarno seemed as bitter a mockery as the mirage of Wilson's Fourteen Points.

Again, while the rest of the world suffered from the "economic blizzard", all other peoples, naturally and necessarily, looked within themselves for the causes of their misfortune. But for the German people, the cause was instantly and unanimously identified as the Treaty of Versailles. For more than a decade, from the very launching of the Paris Settlement, the Germans had been deluged with propaganda setting forth the fact that German recovery and German existence were impossible under the system of the Peace Conference, and now, after ten years, the proof was plain for all to see.

Inevitably, therefore, protest burst forth on all sides. And with equal insistence, millions of voices demanded the abolition of the financial and the territorial prescriptions of Paris, and even the restoration to the Reich of the right to equal armament with its neighbors. But once more, the fatal division of the German people reappeared. On the one hand, a new National-Socialism, which was at bottom no more than the pre-war nationalism in a Fascist disguise, repeated the doctrine of Potsdam; on the other, a rapidly recruiting Communism advocated the principles of Moscow. Thus a whole people, reduced once more to misery, was stirred in its despair by conflicting counsels of violence.

And, in the Autumn of 1930, this counsel produced a new and far reaching political upheaval. On willing ears fell the fiery appeals of the National-Socialists, led by Hitler, a clever demagogue with an amazing popular appeal. The miserable millions heard and believed that salvation was attainable only by the repudiation of a treaty which had been imposed simply as a result of the weakness and folly of German statesmen, and endured solely because of the shameful and corrupt quiescence of cowardly politicians. Reparations were to be abolished, frontiers revised, Germany to be herself again, if only Hitler and his motley crowd were swept into power.

And the Bruening Government, weak and divided, fearful of election returns and itself shaken by the spectacle of national misery, bowed to the storm, and commissioned Treviranus, one of its ministers, to proclaim publicly for it the programme of revision of the eastern frontiers. Even this course failed to break the force of the storm, and in the September election, while the new Nationalists counted more than six millions of votes, the old Communists harvested more than four and a half.

Beyond German frontiers this explosion had consequences doubly disastrous for Germany. On the one hand, Paris, Warsaw and Prague took alarm politically, and on the other, the world, which had adventured its money in the Reich, became fearful for its funds. Thus, while the policy of France and her Polish and Czech allies hardened, the concern of foreign investors led to a rapid withdrawal from

Germany of the vast short term loans, which were the lifeblood of her industrial system.

Yet once more, as in the fatal submarine crisis during the World War, German statesmanship was incapable of calculating the effects of its policy or of appraising the realities abroad. At the bottom of every German mind was the conviction that the whole world was so deeply concerned, alike morally and materially, with the peril to itself of a Red or ruined Reich, that it would perforce intervene to save Germany, once the desperate character of the domestic situation were perceived. The same naïve confidence in the absolute right of Germany to safety, which had moved Bethmann-Hollweg to justify the invasion of Belgium on the ground that Germany was "in a state of necessity" led Bruening and his foreign minister Curtius to a final folly.

Thus, still hard pressed by domestic political opposition, and needing a shining success abroad, Curtius, in March, 1931 put Europe on notice of Austro-German purpose to live within common tariff frontiers. But for France, for Czecho-Slovakia, for Poland, this was the Anschluss. In form and phrase, the proposal borrowed the language of the Zollvereins, which were the preliminary steps to the unification of Germany, as Sadowa and Sedan were the culminating acts.

Nor was this all. The manner of announcing the

project was the manner of Tangier, of Bosnia, of
Agadir. It was precisely the method employed by
Vienna in launching the Serbian ultimatum of
1914. And, in itself, it constituted identically the
same challenge to Paris that the summons to Serbia
had been to St. Petersburg. The whole French system of alliances, the entire prestige of France in
Europe, the security which rested upon both, would
collapse, if this challenge went unanswered. The
Treaty of Versailles, in its territorial, financial and
military provisions would be fatally breached.

But the Germany which issued this challenge
stood, herself, on the very edge of a financial abyss.
The ebb of short time credits, which had begun
with the National-Socialist explosion of September,
1930, had never been completely arrested. German
obligations abroad far exceeded the capacity of the
German banks to liquidate were any sudden demand made for repayment. The whole financial
system, and therefore the economic as well, was a
house of cards. And the defiance to France which
had come from Berlin, was predicated solely upon
the preposterous assumption that the Anglo-Saxon
peoples could and would save Germany from the
consequences of a step, which however to be justified upon moral grounds, and however to be sustained on the basis of purely economic reasons,
politically constituted a declaration of war.

As was always inevitable, the French response to the challenge was swift, sure and devastating. Briand, who might have been president of the Republic, was ignominiously defeated, and his defeat was the advertisement to the world that his country had abandoned his policy, which was the policy of Locarno. At Geneva, French and Czech demands compelled the reference to the World Court of this Austro-German proposal, which, it was alleged, conflicted with treaty and other obligations. But this evasion of the issue did nothing to diminish the unrest which the affair had produced in Europe. On the contrary, from one end of the Continent to the other, it was perceived that Europe was in the presence of what was perhaps the gravest crisis since Serajevo, itself.

And the repercussions of this crisis, financially, were immediate. Almost overnight there began a run on German banks precipitated by the desire of the foreign investors to recover their loans. Confidence, alike in the domestic and foreign circumstances of the Reich, was abolished. Barely more than a hundred days after the challenge of Wilhelmstrasse had gone forth, Bruening and Curtius, Chancellor and Foreign Secretary of the Reich, were in Paris. As Erzberger and Winterfeldt had gone to the Forest of Compiègne to receive the Armistice terms of Foch, these German statesmen now made

a similar hegira to obtain the financial terms of
Laval, the French premier. And in these hundred
days, the measure of time forever associated with
the final act in the Napoleonic drama, Germany
had suffered a disaster as complete as that of
Waterloo.

In vain the President of the United States had
undertaken, by a moratorium applying alike to German reparations and Allied debts, to arrest the ruin
in the Reich. French diplomacy had skilfully postponed the relief while the crash was made unavoidable. And when the crash had come, the restoration
of the financial edifice of Germany seemed dependent alone upon fresh foreign loans, and these were
impossible save by French permission, witnessed
by French participation. For no foreign investors
would risk further loans to Germany while French
political purpose remained unmodified.

But in Paris, as well as London, whither the
statesmen presently journeyed, France confronted
Germany with terms, which on the financial side
were generous, but on the political, usurious. In
fact, she demanded the renunciation by the Reich
of all present purpose to seek revision of the territorial and military clauses of the Treaty of Versailles, in a word to accept the status quo. On the
basis of such a pledge, French milliards were ready;
failing this, French aid was unavailable. Millions

for security but not one sou for charity, that was the French rendering of the old American phrase.

Unlike the Ruhr war, the Battle of the Anschluss did not end with a treaty of peace. There was no immediate "Locarno of the East", such as the French openly sought, because for Bruening surrender abroad was suicide at home. The compromise of London did no more than recognize the enforced stay in Germany of foreign loans which had become frozen and could not be recovered. The Germans returned home empty handed to seek the salvation of the Reich by its own resources. Their hands were free of any new foreign commitment, but if they had not surrendered, neither had the German statesmen succeeded in breaking French resolution, and all the aid which they had received to this end from British and American representatives had been equally unavailing.

And if the Conference of Paris and London had ended in deadlock, and French and German policies remained unmodified, the world was at last confronted by the strength alike of French position and French resolution. As a consequence French prestige in Europe was newly enhanced. By contrast, while Germany had nominally retained her independence of action, actually there was no mistaking the fact that her financial situation left her practically helpless, and that to recover she would,

in the end, be obliged to mortgage her future policy
to foreign lenders. For, only a policy which deliberately avoided conflict, could restore confidence in
the minds of prospective lenders. And of this fact
the humiliating renunciation of the tariff union
by Austria and Germany at Geneva in the following September, was final evidence.

For the third time, then, in thirteen years, Germany emerged crushed from battle with France.
Nor were the conflicts of the Ruhr and the Anschluss less veritably war than the previous collisions,
because no shot was fired in either. The final struggle of the Anschluss had too, disclosed French
power to ruin a Germany seeking territorial revision, and an equal power to prohibit the recovery
of the Germany which had been ruined in the struggle. After the engagement of the Anschluss, Germany was a city besieged, with the lines of supply
all cut, and the resources of the defenders rigidly
limited by a watchful foe.

Yet German purpose remained—and remains—
unshaken, and German policy is still comprehended
in the resolution to suppress the Corridor and realize the Anschluss. In the struggle, German industrial life has been broken at the Ruhr, and German
financial stability shattered in the Anschluss. But
were Germany permitted and assisted to recover
tomorrow, on the next day no one can mistake the

fact that she would turn her strength to the recovery of her eastern frontiers of 1914 at the expense of the Czech and Polish allies of France, and triumph in the east, and expansion at the south, would place hegemony of Europe in her hands and abolish the whole system of security of the French nation. Thus, the issue is unmistakable and it remains unmodified.

No irritation provoked by the ineptitude of German diplomacy, or impatience aroused by the incoherence of German politics should, however, prevent the foreign observer from perceiving the extent and reality of German suffering, and the totally undeserved misery which has fallen to the lot of millions within the Reich. Three times within a brief dozen years the very foundations of confidence and of hope of one of the greatest, most civilized, and in all but politics, most capable of races on this planet, have been shattered. The flight of the Emperor dishonored the régime which he symbolized, the failure of the republic has discredited the system which followed. Faith in justice was shaken by the Treaty of Versailles, and all but destroyed by the occupation of the Ruhr and the crisis of the Anschluss. Beyond all question, the capacity of the German people to endure has been strained almost as dangerously in the post war period as in the years of great conflict itself.

To the German people the alternative seems ever

more completely narrowing down to the choice between the condition of a subject people and the ruin, which has twice flowed from the futile effort to escape from the system of Versailles. And the traveller in the Reich must note with increasing disquiet, the voices raised on every hand celebrating the example of Samson, as indicating the only possible course for a desperate Germany. For deep in the Teutonic soul lies the ineradicable conviction that Germany will not fall alone, nor European civilization long survive her ruin.

Chapter Fifteen

FRANCE

IF GERMAN policy can be summed up in the single word revision, French is similarly comprehended in the term security. Yet what the French actually mean by security is neither quite simple nor by any means self evident. It is not, for example, merely a question of frontiers, armies or limited guarantees. On the contrary, it is primarily a matter of a system. The French desire the establishment in Europe of a system of order. And, quite naturally, their system of order conforms to French conceptions.

The familiar Anglo-Saxon impression that France desires all the world to guarantee her own frontiers, both assumes too much and too little. It is, in fact, the estimate of two isolated peoples confronted by the policy of a Continental state. The French believe that for themselves security can only result from order everywhere in Europe. No channel or ocean interrupts for them the extension of a disorder, which may have its origin upon the banks of the Vistula or the Danube. For America all Europe is remote, for the British, only the western half is adjacent. But the French are compelled to think of the whole continent.

Thus, when a Frenchman talks about security, he is thinking not only of what touches him directly at the Rhine or the Alps, but also and necessarily to what degree he may be affected by something which occurs on the Netze, the Bug or the Tiza. His conception of peace is therefore based upon the idea of a whole continent, not solely of some sort of protection at his frontiers. Americans and Britons equally think of European peace as mainly a Franco-German problem, but both the French and Germans are perfectly aware that their relations with each other will be very largely affected by what happens elsewhere in Europe.

Understanding of French policy in the United States or Britain is made difficult also, because, while there is a very general understanding of French conceptions during the war and immediately after, and a somewhat more limited acquaintance with French policy in the years immediately preceding the great conflict, there is very little knowledge of historical and traditional French policy. And the difference is very profound. Actually since 1919 France has reverted from a state of mind and policy, which date only from the Franco-Prussian War to an older conception. She has, also, resumed the position of a great power, which were partially lost after Waterloo, and wholly after Sedan.

This reversion to tradition has been little appreciated in America, and hardly more widely in England, but by contrast, very fully on the Continent, itself. Americans, therefore, in discussing the French policy of security think mainly in terms of the France, which they knew between 1914 and 1920. They are thinking of an invaded and devastated nation and of the mentality which resulted from these catastrophes. But while the possibility of invasion is never wholly absent from French calculation, it is not today an immediate consideration. In a word, the French are now endeavoring to create a system or order in Europe as a whole, under which they will enjoy security, and not merely to enlist further guarantees for their Rhine frontier. Military guarantee they have in their own resources, but they do not believe that any guarantee, limited to one small corner of Europe, will suffice.

American estimates of contemporary French policy are, too, based upon the period of the Peace Conference and the programme of Clemenceau. But it was only after the disappearance of Father Victory and the collapse of his system, that the present French policy took form. For Clemenceau, although he had been indomitable during the war and had sent defeatists to the firing squad or into

exile, was after all of the generation which had
known Sedan and had lived half of his long life
under the shadow of a dominant and supreme Germany. Even after victory, therefore, he did not believe that France could stand alone. Nor did he
believe discoverable any Continental system which
could permanently withstand Germany, when she
recovered from her defeat.

Thus Clemenceau was not only unimpressed by
Wilson's idealistic programme, which was the
League of Nations, but he was, as well, uncon-
vinced by Foch's prescription of permanent occupation of the left bank of the Rhine. He regarded
the former scheme as Utopian, and the latter as the
vagary of a military mind. For him the single
formula of security was the preservation of the war
time association of his own country with the two
English-speaking nations. When he had, with his
own eyes, seen the French flag again flying above
the cathedrals of Strasbourg and Metz, the remainder of his task was clearly outlined for him.
And he believed he had realized his purpose when
he obtained from Wilson and Lloyd George that
Treaty of Guarantee, which had been the objective
of all of his labors.

Clemenceau's policy was, however, precisely as
contrary to French tradition as Wilson's to American. More successful than his colleague of the Peace

Conference, the French Prime Minister succeeded in forcing it through a reluctant and rebellious parliament. But when the United States Senate rejected the Treaty of Versailles and the Treaty of Guarantee fell with it, Clemenceau's policy was in ruins, and his own political career was at an end. His fellow-countrymen continued to honor him for having saved the victory, but they also condemned him as responsible for having lost the peace.

With the United States gone, and post-war Britain, led by Lloyd George, visibly cooling in its attitude toward its recent ally, it was left to the successors of Clemenceau to construct a new policy in the presence of a Germany, now patently resolved to escape from the frightful conditions of the Treaty of Versailles. This task occupied a little more than a decade extending from the retirement of Clemenceau in 1920 to the great Anschluss Affair in 1931, and in French political history from Millerand to Laval.

It is essential to perceive, however, that the point of departure is the withdrawal of the United States altogether, and the less abrupt, but no less important modification of British policy. France was thus left substantially alone in the presence of an unreconciled Germany, inherently more powerful than herself. She had, at the moment exactly two resources: The Treaty of Versailles, which was the

law of Europe; and a military supremacy due alike
to German disarmament and British demobilization.
The former gave her the right, the latter, the power
to crush any German attempt to evade the Treaty
of Versailles.

In the construction of French policy three men
had considerable rôles. Of the three, Millerand,
who came first, played a part only briefly. By contrast, the contributions of Poincaré and Briand were
decisive. Nevertheless Millerand made one important contribution. Intervening in such measure as
was physically possible, he aided in repelling the
Bolshevist invasion in 1920, and thereafter in the
reconstruction of Poland. Henceforth, France had
an ally. She had saved the Poles, she now became
the guarantor of their existence, and the strong
Polish army, presently to rise, would measurably
replace the Russian on the eastern frontiers of
Germany.

The policy of Millerand found wider extension
under his successors. Czecho-Slovakia, Yugo-Slavia
and Rumania made similar alliances. The Little
Entente became, like Poland, not only a military but
a diplomatic bulwark of French policy. But, on the
other hand, French policy itself was now definitely
embarked upon the defence of the status quo, not
only on the Rhine, but on the Vistula, the Danube
and even the Dniester.

After a brief and inglorious interlude, marked by Briand's humiliation at Washington and disaster at Cannes, Poincaré came to power. The first of his great ministries was noteworthy because of two very definite achievements. At the Conference of Genoa he totally wrecked Lloyd George's ambitious effort to reorganize Europe on behalf of Germany and against France. By the subsequent occupation of the Ruhr, he broke German efforts to evade the Treaty of Versailles. Lloyd George fell soon after Genoa, and Germany temporarily abandoned her resistance to the peace treaty.

Poincaré had now completed the first of his achievements. His fellow-countrymen, too, were becoming restive. They had not welcomed a new mobilization, they had not enjoyed the experience of another war, even within the restricted limits of mere military occupation. And they were disappointed that Poincaré, having promised to collect money from the Germans, had failed. They were ready now to try gentler methods with an enemy who was patently reduced to helplessness again.

The great hour, for which Briand had long watched, was at hand. He had to wait briefly for Herriot to conduct a short lived government, and with MacDonald, to draw the attention of Europe to the all but forgotten League of Nations. But the delay was brief and, all in good time, Briand ar-

rived. In the succession of cabinets of the next few
years, in which he was either Prime Minister or
Foreign Secretary, Briand accomplished one great
feat, he annexed Geneva to France.

What Briand actually did was to transform the
League into what it was always bound in the end to
become, the instrument of a status quo policy. For
the Treaties of the Paris Settlement were the law
of Europe. Without the consent of all of their signa-
tories, they could not be revised save by war. And
the League of Nations existed to prevent war. Thus,
not only legally, but morally as well, peace and the
status quo were inextricably bound up together.

Briand did not invent this manoeuvre. Herriot
and Boncour of France, Benes of Czecho-Slovakia,
Titulescu of Rumania had flaired the opportunity
before the Breton. But it was left to Briand to exploit it. He came, he saw, he conquered at Geneva.
His eloquence, his charm, his genius for dealing
with men, either in conference, or in public assembly, proved irresistible.

When, a little later, the Germans were at last
admitted to the League, they found it garrisoned
by France and her allies. Briand, himself, welcomed
Stresemann in a speech, which filled Europe with
its echoes. The France of Poincaré vanished in the
distance, and the France of Briand replaced it. But
although Germany was now come to Geneva, it was

too late. Poland and the Little Entente were seated in the Council. Briand was literally the Lion of Lake Leman. When he spoke, the Assembly Hall was crowded, what he said was eagerly transmitted to the wide world. The League, as an instrument for procuring treaty revision, was unavailable. Status Quo now reigned in the ancient seat of John Calvin.

Meantime, Poincaré had won his second and greatest struggle, the Battle of the Franc. In the summer of 1926, French finance seemed suddenly to be threatened with the fate of German in the still recent inflation time. And the whole nation, with one voice, recalled the statesman whom it had but recently dismissed with bitter criticism. But while they summoned Poincaré to save the franc, the French people were still content to leave Briand at Geneva, where the sun of Locarno was still shining.

Poincaré's success in restoring the French financial situation was rather a triumph of character than of genius. What had been lacking was confidence, his arrival restored it. In actual operations he was rather driven, than followed, but cautiously, hesitatingly, even reluctantly he took the necessary steps. When his task was completed, France was launched upon a marvelous four years of prosperity. She became what she was long to remain, a

Gibraltar rising above the waves of European bankruptcy.

In saving the finances of France, however, Poincaré had closed the last gap in French armor. During the war, in the early post-war years, France had been under the shadow of Anglo-Saxon finance. She was a debtor nation, and she was compelled to take this fact into consideration in all her actions. That was now ended. The debt settlements had been made and could be met. In fact, to meet them exhausted only half of German reparations payments. The balance went to pay the costs of a reconstruction of the devastated regions which had now been completely reconstructed.

When Tardieu, who had been the lieutenant of Clemenceau, succeeded to power as the heir of Poincaré, the evolution of French policy was already completed. The Treaty of Versailles remained the law of Europe. French military power, still undiminished, was now supported by the rapidly rising armies of her allies, which had been organized by French generals, and supplied by French factories. French financial power had taken its place beside military as one of the foundations of French influence. Finally, Briand's personal ascendancy and French political purposes still prevailed at the League of Nations.

Moreover, although he did not stay long in actual

power, Tardieu added one more detail to French policy. He appreciated the enormous power that came to a nation with a full pocket. He recognized that, if a new occupation of the Ruhr was impossible, the coercion of money might prove more effective and infinitely less expensive than that of men. And between the first and second conferences of The Hague, loans to Britain made his task of negotiating simpler.

Although France had at last emerged from all her difficulties and, in fact, occupied a position of power and prestige unequalled since the Napoleonic epoch, she was already facing a new challenge. British Labor had come to power with a clear mandate to end the Anglo-French Entente, which Briand and Chamberlain had maintained since the great days of the Conference of Locarno. Moreover, across the Atlantic a new American Administration was pressing for disarmament. Presently the world would see Hoover and MacDonald sitting beside the historic waters of the Rapidan and discussing an international programme without reference to France. Finally, Stresemann was dead, and Germany was again in insurrection against the Treaty of Versailles.

The declaration of war was Snowden's insult to the French Finance Minister at the first Hague Conference in 1929. The prelude to the conflict was the

Anglo-American affair at the Rapidan. The first battle was the London Naval Conference. But in this conference Tardieu, serene and sardonic, met the programme of MacDonald and Stimson with an immutable counter-proposition. France would consider naval limitation and reduction provided the United States and Great Britain would consider a guarantee pact in the waters in which France felt herself exposed, namely in the Mediterranean.

Hoover and MacDonald at the Rapidan had not calculated on this. MacDonald had been advised to go, or return, by Paris: Hoover to invite Tardieu or Briand to the Rapidan. The advice had been ignored. At London, British and American statesmen endeavored to undo the consequences of past blunders. But it was too late. The British and American people were unready to give guarantees, the eleventh hour experiments with a consultative pact, were repudiated by Washington. Accordingly, the Five Power Conference failed, and the Three Power Treaty remained conditional. Dreams beside the Rapidan yielded to realities on the banks of the Thames.

The active front now shifted to Germany. In September Treviranus issued his revision pronunciamento: in March, Curtius followed with his Anschluss programme. In the French mind, the Rapidan had been an Anglo-Saxon challenge, the

Anschluss was a German. It was met, swiftly, re-
morselessly, fatally. It was not Tardieu, but Laval,
who welcomed Bruening seeking new Armistice
terms in Paris in July, but the strategy was that of
the man who had served Clemenceau and Poincaré,
and learned from both. Before the ultimate crisis,
too, Washington had intervened. But again the pre-
liminaries had been with London and Berlin, and
not with Paris.

President Hoover sought to save a Germany,
patently in revolt, against the Treaty of Versailles
without the smallest concern for French views. In
fact, he appeared in the Battle of the Anschluss as
unexpectedly as Bluecher at Waterloo. Laval was,
however, more fortunate than Napoleon in dealing
with the unexpected antagonist. Unlike Welling-
ton, Bruening was ruined before aid could become
effective. The ink was hardly dry upon the French
signature to the Moratorium accord, when the financial system of Germany crashed.

France had won another campaign. Germany was
beaten as completely as in the Ruhr affair. Mac-
Donald and Hoover had proven as helpless as
Lloyd George, and Nitti had been before them.
And now the repercussions of the German crash
began to be felt in London, Labor fell abruptly.
The Bank of England appealed to the Bank of
France to assist in the new battle of the pound

sterling, which also failed, when Britain was obliged abruptly to drop the gold standard. The disagreeable financial position France had occupied at the close of the war and in the first post-war years, was now filled by England. Measured in terms of prestige, the results were incalculable.

These results, too, were translated into political forms. At Geneva, Curtius and Schober, for Germany and Austria, renounced the Anschluss a day before the World Court sustained the French case by the narrow margin of 8-7. And concomitantly, not only Austria, but Hungary appeared at the borrower's window of the Bank of France. Bethlen, the Magyar Premier, who had incarnated the cause of territorial revision, abruptly terminated his ten years of power. Moreover, if the renunciation of the Anschluss had been an unparalleled humiliation for Germany, the Hungarian episode was not less clearly a diplomatic defeat for Italy.

France had, then decisively, indubitably won the peace. It had taken ten years. Clemenceau was in his grave, Poincaré had quit public life forever, followed by the admiring gratitude of his fellow countrymen. Briand remained to ring the curtain down upon German disaster and Italian defeat at Geneva. He was, as usual, at his post, and Geneva responded once more to his eloquent appeal for peace—with security. In September, 1931, French power and prestige had attained the utmost limits of the Napoleonic epoch.

But still France had not attained security, and no Frenchman mistook the fact. Six years after Napoleon at Erfurt had displayed a mastery of Europe unrivalled since the days of Charlemagne or of the authentic Caesars, he had been an exile on Elba, and his conquerors were disputing the carcass of his empire at Vienna. It needed but one lost campaign, one colossal disaster to wreck the whole system, which was the Napoleonic prescription for security. And today the situation of the Third Republic abroad is not different.

When the French demand security, therefore, their demand envisages a final dissipation of the challenge which is instinct in German purpose and the danger inherent in Anglo-Saxon policy. The guarantees, which they seek, are for the system which they have established. As a result of the victory of 1918, through the influence of their military power, by the strength of their finance and by the ascendancy of their diplomacy at Geneva, they have position, power, everything except the voluntary submission of Germany, and the equally voluntary association with them of the Anglo-Saxon powers. And they believe to obtain the latter, would be to insure the arrival of the former.

Such is the French theory and system of security.

In this fashion it has developed, and for the present, is supreme. Meantime, what alternative do the Anglo-Saxon powers offer? They propose disarmament, which would remove one of the pillars of the French edifice and discuss revision of the Treaty of Versailles at the expense of Poland and Czecho-Slovakia, which would destroy another. But, in return, they offer nothing but moral exhortation and unsupported forecast of a peaceful Germany.

Both Anglo-Saxon peoples are also, in the main, still unconscious of the nation with which they now have to deal. The United States, in particular, launches all its international undertakings against France. The Washington Conference, the Rapidan colloquy, the Moratorium proposal, all these things were conceived and executed in a manner which literally forced upon the French a policy of opposition, because the obvious, if unintended slight to them, was a matter of comment all over the Continent.

In sum, in the years since the Peace Conference, and as a consequence of Anglo-Saxon policy, France has created a system of order all her own in Europe. It is based upon the peace treaties, which were equally the work of French and Anglo-Saxon statesmen. It is adjusted to the League of Nations, which was not only an Anglo-Saxon creation, but also, remains the single international institution in exist-

ence. In the process of establishing her system,
France has broken every German effort to escape
from the Treaty of Versailles and has repulsed
every Anglo-Saxon attempt to rescue Germany
financially and economically, when such rescue involved manifest peril for the French system, which
is also the law of Europe.

French security, however, still waits upon Anglo-
Saxon recognition of this French system. Once
more, as not infrequently in her long history,
France, seeking security, has found hegemony, but
the brilliance of this achievement does not blind
French eyes to the failure to attain the more practical objective of French policy, which is always
security.

There is, too, one final word, which must be
added. In American and British eyes, French policy
appears an obstinate determination to maintain a
status quo created by victory in war. But the French
are not stupid, and know from their own history
how transitory are all systems of frontiers. In reality,
their policy is not one of status quo, but of balance
of power, and, as such, is the traditional French
policy, which descends at least from the period of
the Thirty Years War.

At bottom, the difference in purpose between
Clemenceau, who advocated the Anglo-Saxon Alliance, Millerand and Poincaré, who constructed the

present system of continental alliances and Briand
and Boncour, who would provide the League of
Nations with force, is very slight. All were equally
concerned in establishing a barrier to a future German domination of the European Continent. All
sought to establish a balance of power against the
strength of eighty millions of Germans living in the
heart of Europe. Clemenceau looked for it in an
Anglo-Saxon guarantee. Poincaré and Millerand
were, perforce, driven to seek it in a system of continental alliances. Briand and Boncour would enlist
the world through the League. But the end in view
is always the same; it is to collect force sufficient to
forbid German hegemony.

The policy of the Anglo-Saxon powers forced
France to substitute her present system of alliances
for the Anglo-Saxon guarantee of the Paris Conference. And the basis of this system of alliances is
the French guarantee of that territorial status quo,
which is essential to the unity of all of her allies,
and to the independence of several of them. But
the task of maintaining this status quo is very far
from popular in France, despite the prestige and
influence which accompany it.

All French policy has, therefore, been comprehended in the attempt to transfer to the League the
responsibility for the territorial circumstances in
Europe, and to furnish the League with power to

deal with any attempt to revise frontiers by force. Were the League to possess adequate power, it could undertake treaty revision, whenever that were possible without war, but its power would constitute a permanent guarantee against any German domination. While the League lacks power, the security of France is, however, indissolubly bound up with the status quo as it affects her allies. But it is utterly to mistake the sentiments of the French people to believe that mere acquisition of prestige reconciles them to playing the rôle of Casabianca on that burning deck of Central Europe, which extends from Gdynia to Ceteta Alba.

Chapter Sixteen

POLAND

THE resurrection of Poland constituted the greatest positive change in the circumstances of the European Continent produced by the World War. In fact this rebirth of Poland, together with the disappearance of the Hapsburg Monarchy, were responsible not alone for transforming the whole Continental situation from the Baltic to the Black Sea, but also for bestowing upon post-war Europe all of its more considerable and difficult problems.

Nothing has, too, contributed more to American and British misapprehension of the European problem than the failure to recognize the enormous consequences of this Polish renaissance. The explanation of this failure is simple. For both of the English-speaking peoples, where their vision is not rigidly limited by salt water, it extends no farther than Berlin, St. Moritz or Venice. Even Vienna, which was once a frontier post of Anglo-Saxon acquaintance and interest, has now disappeared in the fog and confusion of a Balkanized Middle Europe.

Inevitably, therefore, the rights and wrongs, aspirations and ambitions, purposes and policies of the countless millions of men and women belonging to many races, and dwelling in the centre and east of the European Continent, have left Americans and Britons cold, where they have not, indeed, excited irritation and provoked criticism. Beyond the confines of Germany, Switzerland and Italy, only Russia really exists for the Anglo-Saxon world, and Russia, itself, is so variously interpreted, and so ultimately bewildering, that it constitutes a romantic, rather than a political fact, always absorbingly interesting, and invariably colored by mystery and fear alike. Instinctively, they continue to think of the Poles, the Czechs, the Rumanians, the Serbs rather as warlike tribes than as civilized nations. Something of the fashion in which European peoples used once to view the Red Indians of the Far West, is discoverable in American and British views of the peoples of the European Far East.

Thus the states, which have arisen since the World War, have never acquired the definiteness nor the reality of those, which existed in the same regions before 1914. Their personal relation to the problem of peace has been ignored. They have been dismissed as negligible, and the problem, itself, has been narrowly restricted to Franco-German and Franco-Italian issues. As Central Europe has been

Balkanized, all the various peoples have been dismissed with the same contemptuous disapproval bestowed upon the quarrelling tribes below the Danube.

Throughout her brief post-war existence, too, Poland has been handicapped greatly from the inevitable tendency of the Anglo-Saxon world to view her through German eyes. And, for the German people, the rise of Poland from the grave has been, at once, an incredible phenomenon and an incalculable disaster. They could not conceive of such a renaissance, and now that it has taken place, they refuse to credit their senses. Nor are they less instinctively aware that the permanence of Poland constitutes in itself a barrier to all secular German ambitions in the east. Seven centuries of intermittent but tremendous effort at eastern expansion must come to an inglorious end, if Poland survives in anything like her present form.

And, quite sincerely, the Germans believe Polish survival in any such form is impossible, because they think of the Poles as the British were wont to think of the Irish, before the days of the Free State. Polish incapacity to govern is axiomatic in Germany, where this Slavic people are esteemed as artists, but held in contempt from all practical aspects. Equally, the Germans are convinced that Poland cannot and must not survive, save in nar-

rowly restricted circumstances. And this view they
have communicated to both Anglo-Saxon peoples.

The French, on the other hand, have perceived,
not only the fact, but also the very far reaching
consequences of the territorial and political changes,
which have resulted from the World War. They
have gone into the centre and east of Europe to find
a substitute, alike for the Russian ally lost by the
Revolution of 1917, and for the Anglo-Saxon partnership which was terminated after the close of the
great conflict. Confronted by the eternal spectre of
a restored and hostile Germany, they have had recourse to a system of alliance, in which Poland is
the most important detail.

This French policy has aroused bitter German
resentment, which is natural, and a British and
American suspicion, which is a little more difficult
to explain. On the part of the British, it is plain
that criticism of the French system of alliances rises
primarily from an accurate appreciation that in this
fashion France has not only eluded British control,
but has, also in fact, established a system of her
own, which enables her to dominate the Continent,
and at Geneva and elsewhere to checkmate British
purposes. Instinctive British suspicion of all combinations based upon military power, together with
a profound British conviction that the World War

came about because of alliances, largely explain this British hostility.

Again, the deep seated British conviction that the only real prescription for peace in Europe is the placating of Germany, and that such a process must involve the return of the Corridor, plainly runs counter to all Polish interest. It is the fact of Poland which explains the German state of mind to the British. They, therefore, not only resent the fact in itself, but even more angrily condemn the French policy which tends to fortify this fact.

In British eyes, accordingly, Poland has always suffered seriously from the French connection. As far back as 1920, when he was engaged in his duel with France, Lloyd George heard, with unconcealed chagrin, the news of the defeat of the Bolshevist forces before Warsaw, a defeat in which French generals played a rôle. Had Poland been crushed, Lloyd George was satisfied that she could have been deprived of her imperial limits, which were due to the championship of Woodrow Wilson, and compelled to confirm to circumstances which would have been acceptable to the Germans.

The British have, then, measurably accepted the German point of view in respect to Poland. They would willingly agree to a new partition if the result would be a reconciled Germany. They are sharply critical of the French policy, which seeks to consolidate Poland within its present limits, because they hold that this is to perpetuate German unrest and revolt. And German and British opinions have contributed much to the shaping of the American, where the familiar opinion finds support, the opinion that the peace of Europe is conditional upon the suppression of the Polish Corridor.

One other very general impression has developed, namely, that it is simply due to French influence at Warsaw that Poland remains intransigeant on all territorial issues. Thus again, criticism of France is based upon her refusal to exercise authority over a satellite, and to compel Poland to meet German demands. In a word, Poland is dismissed from the question, and the solution of the whole problem is reduced to the simple terms of a Franco-German adjustment in which France, in return for considerations unfixed, shall bring Poland to meet German will.

All of this complicated reasoning, however, ignores one factor, and that is Poland, itself. What has not yet been appreciated sufficiently in Anglo-Saxon countries is that contemporary Poland is not only, in its physical circumstances, potentially a great power, but also that the Poles are traditionally a great people. Unlike all the other Succession states, Poland did constitute a great power over

Baltic
Sea

LITHUANIA

EAST
PRUSSIA

DANZIG
FREE
STATE

SOVIET

GERMANY

P O L A N D

RUSSIA

CZECHO-
SLOVAKIA

AUSTRIA

HUNGARY

ITALY

RUMANIA

YUGO-SLAVIA

Adriatic Sea

BULGARIA

Black Sea

ALBANIA

TURKEY

POLAND
AND THE LITTLE ENTENTE
⦀⦀⦀⦀ States Allied to France

GREECE

Aegean
Sea

long centuries, during which it played a brilliant
and even decisive rôle in European history.

And, although Polish liberty was extinguished by
a coalition of three great empires, Polish literature,
art and culture survived, along with a very clear
national consciousness. In fact, Polish life was
merely suspended, and when the events of 1918
abolished the force which for a century and a half
had restrained Polish national life, it suddenly burst
forth again in all of its traditional vitality and am-
plitude. Moreover, barely come to life, this Poland,
by breaking the invasive power of Bolshevism under the walls of Warsaw, repeated the service of
Sobieski to western civilization, when he similarly
checked Turkish advance before Vienna.

Today, more than thirty millions of people live
within the frontiers of a Polish Republic larger in
area than the British Isles or Italy. Of this population more than two thirds are Polish by race, and
nearly four millions more are Jews, in various
stages of Polonization. The annual increment of
Polish population exceeds that of German. Moreover this state is rich in coal, in timber, in oil and
in agriculture.

The first decade of restored national independence has, too, been marked by an extraordinary economic development. New railways have been built,
old reconstructed to meet national needs, the devas-

tations of the World War have been cleared away, and throughout the country, despite the inescapable consequences of the world wide depression, there has been progress little short of marvellous. In all respects that the eye of the traveller can measure, Poland has already become a going-concern on the economic as on the political side.

Ineradicable German faith in the political and economic incapacity of the Poles, too, has assisted in Polish progress. For, whereas, under normal circumstances the Polish market would inescapably have been dominated by German industry, tariff wars directed against Poland, have forced the Poles to organize an industry of their own, with the aid of French, of American, and even latterly, of British capital, while similarly obliging them to seek markets other than German for their agricultural production. Thus, in resisting German political pressure, they have achieved economic independence.

All of these physical and economic circumstances are, however, merely background, what is decisive is the national will and purpose of the Polish people, themselves. And, here the fact is inescapable. From the moment in which they re-entered into national life, the determination of the Polish people to defend their frontiers, to maintain their unity intact, to resist to death any fresh partition, these have been the dominating impulses of the nation.

This national spirit is the inevitable consequence of history. The record of Polish ruin is written in the story of the partitions. The restoration of the Polish Corridor, which finds favor in Anglo-Saxon eyes, in Polish means only the repetition, on the same territory, of the experiences of Frederick the Great's first mutilation, which was the initial step in the extinction of national independence. What invasion means, in the shaping of French policy, partition signifies in the formation of Polish.

Poland is a nation, then, resolved to fight to the death, rather than consent to any fresh destruction of national unity to satisfy continuing German ambitions. For, in the Polish mind, the question of the Polish Corridor is not contemporaneous but has endured for at least seven centuries. By contrast, it is not difficult to find in Poland, public opinion which considers not impossible some future adjustment between the Poles and the Ukranians, which will involve the reconstruction of the present eastern frontiers. The distinction, however, arises from the fact that in the east, in Volhynia and in Polesia, even in Eastern Galicia, the Poles are a minority, while in Pomerelia, for example, they constitute over ninety percent of the population. Revision, such as the Germans demand, and the British approve, would mean the transfer of upwards of two million Poles to German rule, ten percent of the race inhabiting Europe.

Translated into the terms of the United States, this would mean the sacrifice of more than twelve millions of Americans. Moreover, in the consideration of this aspect of the question, it is necessary to recall all the long history of Prussian oppression of the Polish populations of Posen and Pomerelia, all the bitter struggle alike forcibly to assimilate, and by expropriation laws, to expel the Poles of these frontier regions. It is to such conditions, that the proposal for revision would return two millions of Poles.

It is, then, necessary to dismiss, once for all, the possibility of any peaceful revision of the eastern frontiers of Germany, predicated upon Polish assent, voluntarily given. Today the Polish army has on mobilization a strength of a million. That army is the symbol of national unity, and as such, it is popular as is no other European armed force. It has, too, been organized with the clear appreciation of the fact that defense of national unity is always an impending necessity. And no western mind can quite measure, or comprehend, the passion and determination which are discoverable in Polish patriotism. It is, moreover, well to remember that this patriotism has frequently and in innumerable hopeless struggles against incredible odds, disclosed a willingness to die fighting. And this is the fact which has to be reckoned with in the discussion of peaceful readjustment of boundaries.

There remains the easy assumption that Poland is amenable to French direction or coercion. But, again, no assumption could be palpably more absurd. The Franco-Polish alliance is based on a clear mutuality of interest. French support of Poland is, in a measure, a guarantee of French military and financial aid, in the defense of Polish liberty against German attack. But, by contrast, Polish military strength replaces the lost Russian divisions for a France numerically inferior to Germany. It was the Russian invasion of East Prussia, which by calling two German army corps from west to east, saved the Marne, in 1914. Despite the presence of the British Expeditionary Army on the battlefield, France would have been overwhelmed but for this transfer of troops.

The Polish problem in French eyes, however, goes much more deeply. Unlike the Anglo-Saxon, the Frenchman knows that the Pole will fight. He realizes that words of advice from Paris would not shake Polish purpose, but merely Polish confidence in her ally. But to overwhelm a Polish army, today superior in numbers to the German, would involve re-arming by the Reich. Poland would be beaten in the struggle, but from it Germany would emerge victorious and re-armed. "Do not forget the interesting sequence of Sadowa and Sedan" a Polish Prime Minister said to the French Ambassador at the moment Paris and Berlin were discussing Locarno.

In reality, the Franco-Polish relation is something far different from that of master and satellite. France is bound to Poland as Germany was to Austria in 1914. Into the World War Germany was dragged because she could not stand aside and see her one sure and substantial ally destroyed either by outward attack or inward disintegration. Despite all the incredible stupidities of German statesmanship and diplomacy, the basic fact was that German policy was bound up with Austrian survival.

French security is similarly conditioned. If Poland falls, the whole French system collapses. The Czechs will have no choice but to go to Berlin, the Anschluss will follow automatically. The events of 1866 and 1870 can repeat themselves almost identically. And precisely as long as the Poles are resolved to resist a Fifth Partition of their country by arms, France must support her ally or retire behind the Rhine to await another invasion, which to all French eyes appears, under such circumstances, inevitable.

The fundamental error of both the American and

British public opinions in the matter of Poland, and in fact of all the Succession states, is the result of thinking of these nations as weak in themselves and, in a national sense, inferior peoples and bound therefore to accept the decisions of their more powerful neighbors. That is the old Concert of Europe conception as it was applied to the Balkans. But it broke down in 1912 when the Balkan peoples made war on the Turk against the will of Europe and won their war.

It is, in itself, wholly absurd to think of any nation selling two millions of its citizens into the slavery of an oppressive foreign rule, either to satisfy the anxieties of great peoples to avoid a new conflict, or to gain, for the balance left within national frontiers, a temporary security until the appetite of another power makes necessary another surrender. But all calculations of peaceful revision of the frontiers of Germany in the east are based upon this assumption. And they utterly ignore the reality, which is constituted by the will of a not inconsiderable people to resist to the death a partition, which has many precedents in their own sad history.

Like the French, the Germans know this. Their real calculations of the recovery of the Corridor rest upon future conquest by their own arms alone or future destruction of Poland by a combined German and Russian attack. German policy, in the matter of the Corridor, as distinct from the national will and desire of the mass of the German people for immediate revision, is directed toward preventing the Polish question from becoming stabilized and in creating and sustaining the conviction amongst Anglo-Saxons that French desire for hegemony and Polish intransigeance are responsible for European unrest and German disorder.

But whatever success German policy has had in America or Britain, in Poland it has merely consolidated national spirit and hardened popular will. The resolution to resist is unanimous. Revision means war between Poland and Germany. And even were France to stand aside, which today is unthinkable, the struggle would inevitably extend from the Baltic to the Black Sea and from Italy to the frontier of Soviet Russia. And such a vast upheaval would constitute a strange preface to Peace.

The Germans and the Austrians, in their search for gun fodder to exorcise their crisis in effectives during the war, recalled Poland from the grave. The victors in the war, in conformity with their principle of self-determination, reestablished Poland at the Peace Conference. But today Poland has escaped the control of friend and foe alike. She can be crushed by war. She cannot be partitioned in peace.

Chapter Seventeen

THE LITTLE ENTENTE

As POLAND was the greatest creation of the Paris Peace Conference, the Little Entente has been the most considerable development in post-war Europe. And again, like Poland, the character and inherent strength of this coalition of Czecho-Slovakia, Rumania and Yugo-Slavia has been at once misinterpreted and underestimated by British and American public opinion. As both peoples have refused to see in the rebirth of Poland the restoration of a great power, they have similarly declined to recognize in the Little Entente one of the most considerable elements in the Continental problem.

In its origin the Little Entente was a semi-circle of coercion drawn about a centre of indomitable resistance. In this coalition, the Czechs, the Rumanians and the Serbs were united in the common purpose to resist the aspirations of the Magyars to restore the lost kingdom of St. Stephen by recovering provinces, which at Paris had been distributed amongst the states on the periphery of the sadly shrunken Hungary. Moreover, this primary and fundamental purpose remains a basis of common action and insures the maintenance of a single front in face of Magyar Irredentism by all the states of the Little Entente.

Nevertheless, the nations originally united against a Hungarian renaissance have long ago adopted far more extensive policies and more ambitious purposes. In reality, the Little Entente has politically measureably filled the void which was created in Central Europe by the downfall and disintegration of the Hapsburg Monarchy. And the basis of the policy of this coalition is not merely status quo in the narrower sense of sustaining the Treaty of Trianon against Hungarian attack, but also of preserving the existing situation in all the Danubian region against the attempts of the greater peoples to make it, like the old Balkans, a battle-field of rival great powers.

Measureably, too, this purpose has been realized. All the successive attempts of the Italians to play Austria against Czecho-Slovakia, Hungary against Yugo-Slavia, and Bulgaria against both Yugo-Slavia and Rumania, have come to nothing. Equally unsuccessful have been the efforts of Rome to establish Italian influence in Bucharest, and by direct alliance of Italy and Rumania, to destroy the Little Entente. Manifestly weakened at moments,

this coalition of the three Danubian states has nevertheless endured, and has played a dominating and
stabilizing rôle politically.

Ineluctably, too, the Little Entente policy has
been merged with that of France, and this alliance
itself, has become one of the pillars of French system. Two factors have combined to bring about this
fusion. In the first place, while Italy and Germany
alike, have disruptive policies in respect of the
Danubian area, the French are not only willing but
even eager to see the existing order endure. Again,
common dangers bind the respective states of the
Little Entente to France.

The danger of the Anschluss is for the Czechs
immediate and enduring, and constitutes a threat to
their economic independence and political existence. Against this danger there is no other protection than that to be found in alliance with France,
dominated as she is by the determination to prevent
any further and considerable expansion of German
area and population, which would still further mul-
tiply the odds against herself. In the presence of
German purpose to re-constitute the Mitteleuropa
of the war, the Czechs and French are inevitable
allies.

The Yugo-Slavs, on their part, are faced by an
Italian problem. They have already been compelled
to bow to Italian purpose in the matter of Fiume,

which was not only their natural port upon the
Adriatic, but also assigned to them in the Secret
Treaties of the war era. Nearly a million of their
fellow Slavs dwell within Italian frontiers and are
the victims of a policy of violent assimilation,
which has evoked resistance and produced successive incidents. Alike on the eastern shore of the
Adriatic and in Albania, Yugo-Slav interests and
Italian clash.

But the Italy which is the opponent of the South-
ern Slavs in the Adriatic, is the rival of the French
in the Mediterranean. Fascist imperialism menaces
French security alike in North Africa and in the
Maritime Alps. Common dangers at the Isonzo and
the Roya, therefore, serve as a solid foundation for
Franco-Slav alliance. On a smaller scale, and in relation to Italy, the alliance between Belgrade and
Paris recalls the pre-war association between St.
Petersburg and Paris. And for Yugo-Slavia and
Czecho-Slovakia, French financial resources are as
precious as their own military forces are essential
to France.

Between Rumania and France, the basis of association is not direct. But in the east, the smaller
Latin state faces precisely the same danger as Poland. In fact, Soviet purpose to recover Bessarabia
has never been disguised, while, at least for the
present, Bolshevist Russia has accepted the terms of

the Treaty of Riga as definitive. Poland, then, is Rumania's only possible ally against an uncompromising foe. Inevitably, therefore, Bucharest and Warsaw have, in their turn, struck hands in a defensive alliance. But since Poland is an ally of France, as are Czecho-Slovakia and Yugo-Slavia, all Rumanian associations tend to bring her in closest contact with France, while her financial necessities compel her to apply to Paris.

The nations of the Little Entente are, therefore, bound to France, not only by their common policy, which is the maintenance of the status quo in the Danubian area, created at the expense of both Hungary and Bulgaria, but also by their separate and special circumstances which similarly throw them into the French system. Thus, from the moment of its formation, the Little Entente has been a partner in French policy, as has Poland.

Yet, once more, it is necessary to perceive the foundations of this partnership. In western eyes these various states are regarded as jerrybuilt edifices, without national cohesion or political solidity. There is widespread conviction that they are no more than puppets dancing at the end of a string pulled in Paris and that, like Poland, they are intransigeant, not because of any parochial circumstances but primarily because French interest is served by this spirit.

But, again, no calculation could be more inexact. Collectively these three states number nearly forty-five millions of inhabitants, more indeed than the total of Italy or of France. Their combined military strength on mobilization exceeds that of any great power, with the possible exception of Soviet Russia. And each of the three peoples, united by the agreements of the Little Entente, is, like the Polish, not alone inspired by the determination to exist, but also dominated by recollection of recent division and secular oppression. Nor is it less clear that, even if the Hungarian peril is for the present far from formidable in the face of the overwhelming resources of the Little Entente, for the Czechs and the Serbs, German and Italian purposes are respectively deadly challenges.

If, however, France were to attempt at Prague or at Belgrade, to urge a policy of compromise and sacrifice, surrender on the part of the Czechs to the projected union of Austria and Germany, concession on the part of all nations within the Little Entente to Hungary, modification of Yugo-Slav aspirations in the face of Italy in the Adriatic, then for these peoples the French alliance would lose the single value which it possesses. Then they would turn to Berlin or Rome to make their own terms.

As the situation stands, in return for her support of the existing order and the policies of her allies of

the Little Entente, France received unmistakable
payment. Czecho-Slovakia stands as a formidable
obstacle to German expansion down the Danube.
Yugo-Slavia is prepared to march with France in
any conflict between Rome and Paris. And Rumania, for her part, constitutes at least a theoreti-
cally useful ally for Poland, in the face of a Russian menace always unmistakable.

At Geneva, too, French diplomacy, so far from
being isolated in the face of the Germans, the Italians, and the Anglo-Saxons, finds herself at once
supported alike by Polish and Little Entente ministers. And in Benes and Titulescu, Briand has
found his most valuable and effective assistants in
his long and successful assertion of French supremacy in the League of Nations. Deprived of this
support, the French position would be as little brilliant as the Italian, for French isolation would be
at least as complete.

French security, too, would be as utterly compromised as French influence and prestige, were the
present system of alliance to collapse. As Napoleon,
after Leipsic, was condemned to seek vainly to defend France on French soil, following the collapse
of all his system of alliances, French statesmanship
would be thrown back upon national resources
alone, were the Little Entente to disintegrate, and
Poland to be broken to German will. On the other

hand, all of these exposed and relatively weak nations might sink to something of the level of the several Balkan states, before 1914.

Like the Franco-Polish alliance, therefore, the partnership between the Little Entente and France is also based upon a mutuality of interests, and there is little to suggest the relation between satellite and superior. The position of France in Europe, and in the world, is dependent upon the support of her eastern allies. But even more unmistakable is the fact that the security of France is also conditioned upon this association. French profit from the combination is therefore incalculable, but French responsibilities and French policy are similarly regulated in no small measure by the purposes and perils of her associates.

Unmistakably, too, this infinitely complicated system of alliance has at least one obvious and grave defect. It is founded, not upon economic, but political facts. In this respect it might almost be said to be an alliance against nature, itself. For the considerations of trade and commerce, the circumstances of agriculture and industry alike, dictate the close association of all the peoples of the Central European area from Hamburg to Salonica, and from Trieste at least to the frontiers of Soviet Russia. The dissolution of the economic bonds, which united the larger portion of this area within the

Hapsburg Monarchy was a disaster without limit for the whole Continent.

Politically, the interests of all the peoples of the Little Entente are with Paris, but economically all are unmistakably, and even almost irresistibly, drawn into the orbits of Berlin and Vienna. It is the German and Austrian markets in which Yugo-Slavia and Rumania would naturally sell their agricultural products, and from them that they would draw their industrial supplies and factory-made goods. In this region France sells little and buys less. She can lend her allies money, but she cannot absorb their products. And loans are a transitory episode; markets, a continuing necessity.

French policy has labored continuously, therefore, to find an economic base for a political association, which is of utmost importance to herself. But in the main, it has failed because the opposing forces have been too strong for her. The Austrians have continued to look to Germany, the Hungarians have remained resolute in their passive resistance to a system of frontiers against which they have no present power to revolt. Italy has endeavored constantly to prevent the reincarnation of a new Danubian confederation recalling, at least on the economic side, the old Hapsburg Monarchy and bound, under present conditions, to look to Paris and not to Rome.

Europe, then, has been treated to the impressive paradox of a political alliance continuing to function, and even acquiring added strength, while the constituent nations have visibly suffered economic hardships because of their political policies. On the economic side, there are but two conceivable formulas for the restoration of prosperity in the Danubian area, either the expansion of German tariff limits through the creation of a new Mitteleuropa, or the restoration of the old associations of the peoples who once made up the Hapsburg Monarchy. But the first solution would be ruinous for the Czechs, while the second is impossible without the voluntary participation of both Austria and Hungary. And the Austrians visibly prefer union with the Reich while the Hungarians remain resolved to recover their lost provinces.

Against the German solution all French policy instinctively and naturally reacts. Toward the formula of a restored Austro-Hungarian association, by contrast, French opinion is unmistakably turning, increasingly. All French interests would be best served thereby. In fact, it is the only escape Paris can discover from the alternative of universal ruin or German economic and political domination in the Danubian area. But while France can, in a crisis like the Anschluss, rely upon Italian resistance to the prospectus of Pan-Germanism, she is also con-

demned to encounter Italian, as well as German
hostility, to the alternative project.

The industrially and commercially minded
Anglo-Saxons, impressed by the economic ruin
which exists and spreads in all of Central Europe,
have easily and generally surrendered to the German solution. And, as a consequence, they view
with impatience and irritation, the whole French
system of alliances and, in particular, the pretensions of the Little Entente to the role of a great
power. Conviction as to the means of ending an
intolerable economic condition, has, however,
blinded both American and British opinion to the
strength of the obstacles in the pathway of any
such project and produced a total miscalculation of
the political factors involved.

For France and Italy, alike, the German solution
would mean the decline to the condition of a second class power and while French security would
again be compromised at the Rhine, Italian would
be imperilled from the Quarnero to the Isonzo.
Strasbourg and Metz on the one hand, Trieste and
Pola on the other, would automatically be endangered. Czecho-Slovakia would be threatened by extinction. But, by contrast, Yugo-Slavia and Rumania might in the end be advantaged, provided
Germany were militarily strong enough to guaran-

tee the Yugo-Slavs against Italy, and financially as well as militarily, sustain the Rumanians.

The Little Entente, therefore, constitutes the single barrier to Pan-German domination in Central Europe. As a consequence, it is one of the pillars of French policy as Poland is the other. But, as in the case of Poland, French policy is far more the captive than the master of its allies. For the present, France and the Little Entente—and Poland as well —must stand or fall together.

Precarious this system of alliances patently is, but no alternative is discoverable. Least of all is the British and American prescription applicable. For that amounts to subordinating politics to economics. Such a course would be ruinous for the peoples who today possess power and immeasureably advantageous for the nations, which are helpless but still hold the keys to the economic situation.

A purely economic solution of the Central European problem would give Germany a political situation unequalled since the early days of the Holy Roman Empire. A purely political solution, which is the present prescription, can easily spread ruin from the Baltic at least to the old Balkans. Such is the complicated situation in Central Europe, where the Little Entente, as the ally of France, exercises absolute power without any present prospect of providing even moderate prosperity.

Chapter Eighteen

GREAT BRITAIN

Post-war Britain presents a fairly bewildering array of contradictions. It is a nation which, although victorious in battle, unmistakably lost the war. Traditionally and inherently a great power, it is today, alike physically and morally, unable to play its historic rôle. Finally, although still a rich empire, it has been forced to borrow from a less favored rival to protect its own currency.

The explanation of all these paradoxes is, of course, found in the fact that the World War surprised the British people on the threshold of a domestic social revolution. The conflict itself accentuated the pace of this domestic upheaval. Last of all, the political transformations within the empire and the profound modifications in the financial, industrial and commercial circumstances of the whole world since 1919 have combined to intensify a crisis, which had in fact, begun before the Assassination of Serajevo.

As a consequence of this varied and far reaching

dislocation of the very foundations alike of British prosperity and power, it is today quite impossible to foresee whether the Britain of the latter half of the Twentieth Century will still be a world empire or little more than another Holland; whether it will decline to the rank of a second class European power or recover that unrivalled position which it occupied in the closing decade of the last century. All that is plain at the present hour is that it has become practically a negligible quantity politically in contemporary Europe, with consequences at least as disastrous for the Continent as for itself.

The evidence of the decline of British power is disclosed in the complete failure of British policy to achieve any of its ends in the years between the Armistice and the fall of the second Labor Government. That policy was at once obvious and traditional. At the close of the World War, as at the end of all previous continental struggles in which England had been engaged, British political and economic interests were alike concerned in the prompt restoration of peace and prosperity in Europe, and in the preservation of the balance of power on the Continent.

As a trading and banking people, the British were bound to be affected by any prolongation of the prostration which had accompanied the great conflict. "Business as usual" was the essential re-

quirement of a nation which had been forced by
the circumstances of the struggle to undertake a
burden of debt unprecedented in human history.
Nor had anything in the present era changed the
time-honored British interest in preventing the
domination of the Continent by a single nation,
whose supremacy rested upon military circumstances alone.

With Germany defeated and disarmed, Austria
dissolved, and Russia disappearing in the red haze
of Bolshevism, nothing was more certain than that
British interest would find itself confronted by a
France almost miraculously restored to that position which it had occupied from the rise of Louis
XIV to the fall of Napoleon Bonaparte. Thus, the
ally of the war was predestined to become the rival
of peace, and Britain was condemned in advance
to seek to restrain the influence of France until such
time as the European states themselves, recovering
from the immediate effects of the conflict, could
establish a new system of balance of power.

But all British effort to pursue her accustomed
course in the post-war years led to complete frustra-
tion. Twelve years after the Armistice, on the one
hand, the hegemony of France was beyond question or challenge, and on the other, the economic
and financial prostration of Central Europe was
hardly less complete than at the moment the Paris

Conference completed its labors. Moreover, from all the conflicts of French and British policies, France had emerged successful with her purpose, if not yet fully realized, still unshaken.

The reasons for this British failure are many and varied. They are at once moral and material, political and economic, and no single cause explains the unmistakable fact. It is clear, however, that the World War produced a far reaching psychological effect upon the British mind. At its close, the whole population of the British Isles was disillusioned, embittered, dominated by the desire to escape from European entanglements which had brought only unimaginable disaster. The very thought of war had become abhorrent, the distrust of the ally was hardly less profound than the antagonism for the enemy. The British people were eager to cut their losses and have done with the whole complicated and costly European mess. Demobilization of foreign policy was just as urgently demanded as demobilization of the vast armies, which the war had called into being.

As a consequence, the British people, with amazing swiftness, swept away their huge military establishment. From one of the greatest military powers, Britain declined to the rank of a Succession State in a few brief months. But when this transformation had taken place, a voluntarily disarmed

Britain was actually almost as destitute of power as a forcibly disarmed Germany.

At the Paris Conference, too, British statesmanship made a fatal blunder, from the consequences of which British policy has suffered continuously ever since. Having in the notorious Khaki Election promised the British masses to make Germany pay the last farthing of the war costs, Lloyd George at Paris insisted upon imposing impossible reparations. And, despite British protest, and thanks to Woodrow Wilson, there were also written into the Treaty of Versailles territorial conditions which were similarly intolerable to the German mind.

But these territorial conditions were immediately and increasingly the foundation of national policy in the minds of the French people. And the reparations obligations, impossible as they appeared, could be reduced only with French consent. To save Germany from the financial and the psychological consequences of these astronomical impositions, indeed, to save Germany on any terms, was the very basis of British policy and interest, but in accepting the Treaty of Versailles, British statesmanship had placed all legal weapons in French hands, and in disbanding British armies, had abolished all power to restrain French action.

This fact was fully disclosed in the years following immediately upon the Paris Conference, when

Lloyd George undertook to engage in a duel with France with the purpose of saving Germany alike from the consequences of her own blunders, and of French coercion. But when, after Lloyd George, himself, had fallen as a result of the visible bankruptcy of his policy and French armies marched into the Ruhr in defiance of British will, the weakness of England was revealed. For in that crisis, the nation, which had sent the Mediterranean fleet through the Dardanelles at the moment of San Stefano, and started Kitchener up the Nile in the hour of Fashoda, was condemned to limit its protests to the shrill scoldings of Curzon, which only moved Poincaré to dialectical masterpieces.

The failure of the Lloyd Georgian policy of opposition to France led to the substitution by the Tories of the old order of the Entente Cordiale. Locarno presently came to give a brief promise of European tranquillity, and for several years Briand, Chamberlain and Stresemann met at Geneva, and coöperated in the task of restoring European order. And in these years, from 1925 to 1929, the progress of Europe towards peace was striking in the extreme.

Nevertheless, beneath the surface, British public opinion stirred uneasily. In the Locarno pacts, France had at last obtained British guarantee for the status quo in the west. But it was plain that this was not enough. At Geneva, everywhere, French statesmen still demanded that the whole system of Paris be stabilized for all present time by mutual guarantees and, above all, by British promises to respect and aid in the preservation of the status quo.

Such pretensions seemed, to the British mind, intolerable. The British people were satisfied that they had saved the French during the war, and assumed fresh responsibility for the security of France in the Locarno pacts; that, in addition, they had made vast sacrifices in the matter of French debts to Britain. These concessions and sacrifices, so it seemed to the British masses, had only served to whet French appetite. Moreover, the continuing strength of French armies, the unmistakable strength of French air fleets, the growing French activities in naval construction, all touched the old but not yet extinct suspicion of the neighbor beyond the Channel, which had survived from the age of Napoleon.

All of these details and many others contributed to the defeat of the Tory Government in the election of 1929. And, while in this campaign, domestic economic questions outweighed considerations of foreign policy, and even in foreign policy, Tory intransigeance toward the United States in naval questions was more unpopular than alleged truckling to France, it was not less clear that the British public listened with approval to the Labor and Liberal speakers indicting Chamberlain as the tool of Briand, and condemning a foreign policy, which made Britain the passive agent of France.

MacDonald came to power for a second time, with a clear mandate to break the ties with Paris. For him and for his followers, too, there was an almost equal eagerness to substitute the German for the French partner. The decisive step was taken by Snowden at the Hague Conference and, for the moment, all Britain broke into applause at the Chancellor of the Exchequer's resounding negative to further French demands. And with that response, the Entente Cordiale lapsed again.

But while it was easy to be off with French friendship, it was less simple to realize Labor purposes in the face of a hostile France. Thus French action at the London Naval Conference presently made impossible a Five Power Treaty, and reduced to insignificant proportions the harvest of an international meeting upon the success of which Labor had counted heavily. Moreover, at Geneva and elsewhere, Labor's plans for disarmament, for coöperation, and confidence, were systematically and completely brought to nothing by French opposition. For Paris, London under Labor rule, had become an enemy capital, and British policy as hostile as German.

The great financial crisis of the summer of 1931, moreover, exposed the utter bankruptcy of Labor policy. The collapse of German finance under French attack, which was both political and monetary, brought the Reich to the edge of ruin, and the British Prime Minister, by means of the Paris and London Conferences, sought to move French resolution. But, in vain; France was now tasting the delights of victory after battle and met MacDonald's emotional appeals with calm and remorseless logic. French money would be loaned to the Reich only on French political terms. The way to the French stocking was through renunciation of the policy of revision.

Failing to obtain French aid, MacDonald made a dramatic flight to Berlin to carry assurances of British sympathy and support for the Bruening Cabinet. But he returned to London to find the pound sterling faltering under French withdrawals. And, while the Labor Cabinet divided and broke up, the Bank of England had presently to turn to Paris as well as to New York for financial assistance which proved unavailing. Thus, two years after Labor had set out confidently to raise the alleged French mortgage upon British foreign policy and to rescue Germany from French coercion, Germany was broken and Britain was in grave trouble. Nor could the temporary survival of MacDonald in a National

Cabinet, disguise the extent of his failure. Like Lloyd George, he had set out to break French hold upon the Continent, and like the Welshman, the Scot had, in his turn, met shattering defeat.

After as before the financial crisis, British public opinion remains unchanged. Faithful to the tradition of their race, the English are concerned with finding a course of expediency to end the present Continental conflict. For them the problem of peace is exclusively the task of discovering some basis of adjustment between France and Germany. Thus, with sound instinct, but with undisguised reluctance, they undertook to satisfy French demands for security by subscribing to the Locarno pacts. But in this guarantee of the status quo on the Rhine, they conceive full justice has been done to the legitimate French claims.

By contrast, German claims remain. Satisfaction for these, too, is discoverable only through the revision of the territorial provisions of the Treaty of Versailles. As a consequence, the British would approve the suppression of the Polish Corridor, and would similarly assent to the Anschluss, because they see clearly that German resolution in respect of these issues is as fixed as French in the matter of security. As for the rights of the Poles or the Czechs, for them they display the same supreme un-

concern that Sir Edward Grey disclosed for Serbia
in the early phase of the Serajevo crisis.

As to the French conception of a system of peace
covered by general guarantee of the whole status
quo of the peace treaties, this, in British eyes seems
no more than the purpose to continue the war, to
keep Germany down, to repeat the course, which
Germany herself followed in respect of France and
over Alsace-Lorraine after 1870. Once the frontiers
of France were covered by a British guarantee,
French concern for Polish rights or for Czech security appeared in British eyes equally unreasonable
and even ungrateful.

The fundamental selfishness of this British view,
disclosed in a willingness to sacrifice Poland, is justified at home by the conviction that Poland cannot
permanently hold the Corridor and therefore, as a
counsel of prudence, should come to terms with her
greater neighbor. And the cloak of idealism is cast
over this rather hard realism, by the citation of the
fact that the inescapable alternative is another general war. The price of European peace, to the British mind, is the placating of Germany, and Britain
advocates paying the price, just as, from her own
point of view, she has already paid the price of
French security in the Locarno pacts.

The fatal weakness of this British policy of expediency lies in the fact that Britain no longer has

power or influence to impose it. She has alternately opposed the French and sought to win them by concessions, which however insufficient in French eyes, bulk large in British. But both courses have failed. Lloyd George and Ramsay MacDonald were equally unlucky in the attempts at opposition while Austen Chamberlain roused British protest without completely satisfying French demands. And if MacDonald's failure should be followed by a new reversion to the Entente Cordiale, it will not only constitute an immediate humiliation but must also in the end run counter to the deep-seated British conviction that French policy, which is repugnant to England, is also ruinous for Europe.

All the contrasting genius of the two races is revealed in their prescriptions of peace. For France, the solution is an elaborate and rigid system of law sustained by force. For the British, the answer is found in a series of improvisations and adjustments, proceeding continuously and made possible by enduring common sense. The French insist that the British shall join with them in enforcing the law; the British seek to persuade the French to make compromises which shall render law enforcement unnecessary. As the French have been the stronger in recent years, they have extorted a measure of British assent. But this assent has been grudging,

and since it has been made against conviction, it has
often been withdrawn. And, in fact, the national
policies of the two peoples are, at bottom, no more
easily to be reconciled than the French and
German.

Chapter Nineteen

ITALY

IF BRITISH interest is not directly engaged on either side of the debate over status quo and revision, Italian, characteristically enough, is enlisted on both sides. For the Italians are a Status Quo people in the matter of the territories which they acquired through the peace treaties and a Revision power for what they failed to get. Mussolini has affirmed that the basic doctrine of Italian policy is "nothing for nothing." But, in fact, it is "something for nothing."

From the World War, Italy emerged more disappointed than any other Continental state belonging to the victorious coalition, and more disillusioned than any country save Britain. She had recovered Italia Irredenta; Trieste and the Trentino were now new jewels in the Crown of Savoy. Her age-long dream of security had been realized at the Brenner, but otherwise her situation was little changed.

After 1919, as before, Italy was a second class state with the aspirations and appetites of a great power. Great Britain and France had expanded their colonial empires. Even Belgium had acquired provinces on the borders of her Congo Empire, but abroad, Italy remained where she had stood in 1914, her overseas empire limited to the Tripolitan and Erythean façades to barren hinterlands. And these desert possessions, representing vast costs in blood and treasure, were set in immediate and vivid contrast to a French Empire, which on the Mediterranean included Tunis, Algeria and Morocco, and extended inland to the Niger and the Congo.

Beyond the Isonzo, the Hapsburg Monarchy had disintegrated, but in its place had risen a large and virile Yugo-Slavia. In Anatolia the dream of an Italian sphere of influence had fallen swiftly before the power of Kemal Pasha, although in adjoining Syria, French power was seated alike at Beirut and at Damascus. In Central Europe the development of the Little Entente quickly closed the door to Italian influence. Even on her own frontiers Italy was presently confronted by a military alliance between France and Yugo-Slavia, while in all international meetings, the association of Poland and the Little Entente with France, reduced Italian influence to zero.

Isolated, Italy could do nothing. But where was she to find an ally? Berlin was cold and unresponsive alike because German statesmen remembered

the desertion of 1915, and German soldiers, mind-
ful of Caporetto, placed little value upon an Italian
military alliance which involved collision with the
French army. Always, too, Wilhelmstrasse was
dominated by the conviction that the Italian proposals were no more than a detail in a scheme to
obtain German agreements only to sell them at a
good market to the Quai d' Orsay.

In the southeast Rome sought a partner in
Bucharest, but although Rumania occasionally in-
clined to Italy, French money and Little Entente
influence always brought Italian intrigue to nothing. Hungary offered a better field for activity, and
Rome and Budapest, during the régime of Bethlen,
gave many outward evidences of a secret understanding. But in the end, the economic and financial
weakness of Hungary brought about Bethlen's resignation and his successor Karolyi took office to accept a French loan on French political terms.

In the pre-Fascist days Nitti played with Lloyd
George against France. But the Genoa Conference
ruined Lloyd George and counted as a decisive triumph for Poincaré, which was soon followed by
the occupation of the Ruhr. When Mussolini arrived, Nitti disappeared first in prison and then,
after a sensational escape, to a retirement, from
which he issued endless denunciations of French

policy, but out of office he proved as futile as he had been helpless in power.

Fascist foreign policy took up the problem with new hopes but with no fresh resources. The adventure of Corfu was a moral disaster without the smallest compensation in prestige. Labor England was utterly hostile to Fascism and Tory statesmen were the frank advocates of the Entente Cordiale with France. In Germany, the Social Democrats and the Roman Catholic Centre were equally unfriendly to Fascism, while Stresemann heard with ill-concealed indignation the appeals of the German-speaking population of the Southern Tyrol, provoked by a ferocious policy of Italianization.

To the ever bitterer Italian threats, France presently replied by massing divisions on the Alpine frontier from Menton to Mont Cenis, and by financing, not alone the military, but also the naval programme of Yugo-Slavia. French-built submarines appeared at Cattaro on the track of Italian commerce between Trieste and the open sea. French-built airplanes watched the Italian frontier from Gorizia to Fiume. Concomitantly the economic and financial necessities of the Fascist regime compelled it to put a limit to fiery speeches which disturbed world confidence.

Throughout the post-war years, while France grew visibly stronger, Fascist Italy became more

violently resentful. The passion was due alike to
the inherent rivalries between the peoples and to
the undisguised hostility of a republican France to
a Fascist Italy. The neo-Napoleonism of the Duce
aroused sympathy only in a very limited section of
French public opinion. As a consequence, the
myriad of Italian exiles, forced to flee before the
Fascist régime, found ready asylum on French soil
and beyond question used their new home as a base
for intrigue and attack beyond the Alps.

Presently Italian policy came down upon naval
parity with France as the issue of battle. Such parity
in battleships had been obtained in the Washington
Naval Conference. But all effort to extend this
equality to other categories failed at Geneva and
London. Aroused by Italian threats, fearful of her
exposed situation in the Mediterranean, where the
line of communications between Marseilles and
Tunis, Algiers and Oran was vital, France resisted
all Italian demands.

Eager to enlist Anglo-Saxon support, Italy
adopted the programme of disarmament which
found its chief advocates in President Hoover in
America and Prime Minister MacDonald in Britain.
But the French easily penetrated the design. For
parity was attainable for Italy only as navies were
reduced greatly, since the French purse was long
and the Italian lean. And, France, backed by her

Continental allies, had no difficulty in mastering Italian manoeuvres at Geneva.

The great economic depression of 1931, moreover, exposed the total weakness of the Italian situation. Like Germany, she was incapable of making any successful financial stand against France. A poor country, without large accumulations of capital, lacking in raw materials, condemned to buy food abroad, Italy appeared only as a passive spectator in the great conferences of Paris and London, where the fate of Germany was at stake. And the same situation brought to nothing all her combinations in Central Europe, since Vienna and Budapest were compelled to make application for financial aid at Paris and accept the political conditions, which were inevitably attached to these loans.

Even in the Anschluss crisis, which preceded the financial crash, Italy's situation was anomalous. Her desire for close relations with Berlin was clear, but the danger for her of any Austro-German combinations, was equally patent. Trieste and Meran, even more than Strasbourg and Metz, would be immediately endangered, and no British guarantee covered the Italian frontier cities, as it did the French. Mussolini could leave to Briand the unpleasant task of open opposition, but he could not give Bruening and Curtius that aid which would alone incline them to an Italian association. Nor was the Italian judge on the bench of the World Court able to escape voting with the French and thereby casting the decisive ballot to pronounce the Austro-German tariff union illegal.

Italy was then caught and she remains caught. She has the ambition and self-confidence of a giant, she has a faith in her power and in her force which surpasses that of any other nation. Her population of forty-two millions, already above that of metropolitan France, is growing at a far faster rate. Her manpower exceeds that of her rival, but all other advantages are in the hands of the nation beyond the Alps.

Strategically, she is equally at the mercy of French seapower seated at Toulon, Corsica and Bizerta and British, based upon Gibraltar, Malta and Suez. Her great cities are exposed to air attacks coming from east and west alike, and originating at Cattaro or Bastia. Her ambitions in the matter of Tunis awaken only apprehension in the British Admiralty, where there is no desire to see Italy seated on either shore of the narrow strait connecting the two halves of the Middle Sea. Financially, she is incapable of supporting either military or naval establishments equal to the French. As an ally, she can offer little but an exposed situation, which would make her rather a liability than an asset.

Nevertheless, in their present state of mind, the

Italian people are in a condition of moral revolt against their physical circumstances. Fascism is a frank gospel of unashamed imperialism, Italian policy is the only undisguised example of the once familiar *realpolitik*, the policy of force now extant. The prospect of a New Rome is perpetually held out before the eyes of the rising generation, which is being educated as the heir of the old. But the patrimony of the Caesars has been distributed. France is master in North Africa, and Britain holds the Mediterranean, not only at Gibraltar and Suez, but also at Malta.

The Italian phenomenon is, then, one of the most disturbing in contemporary Europe. The Anglo-Saxon nations have been content to dismiss it with a certain condescension, accepting the passionate prospectuses of Mussolini as directed at home audiences and calculated only to satisfy a people, which lacks the capacity to disturb world peace. And, along with this comfortable optimism goes the cheerful assumption that Fascism is a form of domestic discipline good for Italians although, of course, impossible for more serious peoples.

Yet Fascism is a force, and Fascist Italy a factor, which cannot be so lightly dismissed in the consideration of the Europe of the future. Today, the activities of the Black Shirts are mainly confined to

domestic organization, which finds widespread applause in America. Yet if, at the present time, the
people who profess this doctrine of force are powerless to translate it into action, they are continuously and consciously preparing for a tomorrow, in
which they believe the strength of fifty millions will
compel a re-ordering of frontiers and a redistribu-
tion of colonial territories and raw materials alike.

Nor is the fact to be mistaken that the objectives
of Fascist ambition are attainable only by conflict.
Italian nationalism is a religion of war. Italian
claims to territorial revision have no basis in the
ethnic character of populations and no such defense
of them is urged. No question of national unity or
of strategic security explains Italian demands as it
does German or French. Geographically, Italy has
a frontier more nearly impregnable than France
could acquire, even if she occupied the Rhine perpetually. The single conceivable menace, that originating in Yugo-Slav aspirations, is of itself insignificant, given the relative numbers of the two
peoples.

Not liberty, not unity, not security, the objectives
of all other peoples and the basic explanation of
their national policies, is at stake in the Italian case,
only power. The right to a place in the sun, the old
and once familiar demand of Pan-Germanism, in-

spires Italian policy and Fascist purpose. To the
Italians themselves, this clear and unequivocal assertion of national purpose seems not an evidence
of a spirit distinct from that of all other European
nations, but rather the proof of an honesty in the
face of universal hypocrisy. And here again the re-
semblance between pre-war Pan-Germanism and
post-war Fascism is impressive.

In any event, Italian policy is unmistakable. The
purpose of the men and the party today dominant
in the Peninsula is to exploit every political development on the Continent to the greater glory of
Italy, and to the expansion of Italian prestige and
power. In this purpose Italy may today side with
Germany and tomorrow with Soviet Russia, she may
support an American project for disarmament, or a
German for military equality with France, but with
her statesmen, the value of the principle endorsed
lies purely in the profit it may yield to Italy in the
immediate present.

In the capital of no other great people which engaged in the World War, does one hear discussion
of the next war in the same tone as in Rome. In no
other country is the press, public opinion, national
life, similarly regimented and disciplined in deliberate anticipation of a new conflict. Everywhere else
on the Continent the voice of pre-war imperialism

has been modified, but in Rome the example of the
Caesars is an inspiration to a contemporary gospel
in which the lessons of 1914-18 have no place. Today the basis of Italian policy is opportunism, but
in all Italian minds this is but a stage.

Chapter Twenty

RUSSIA

SOVIET Russia is a state dedicated to the cause of World Revolution but, because of its present necessities, condemned to seek peace with its enemies. Moscow strives constantly to conduct ordinary diplomatic negotiations with capitalistic countries, but, at the same time, it cannot for a moment renounce its purpose to promote domestic revolution within their frontiers. Its fundamental principle is based upon class warfare, its present foreign policy is conceived in the idea of international tranquillity.

Not unnaturally governments and peoples find it difficult to discover a basis for normal relations with the Soviet Union in the face of this paradox. How to be at peace with a nation which is at war with the world? This is the conundrum for the statesmen of all other countries. The puzzle is made more intricate, because in the brief years of its existence the Soviet Union has had not one, but three policies. Immediately following 1917 the Bolshevists were on the defensive. They were compelled to defend themselves against attacks of Czarist generals and admirals backed by Allied resources and troops. This defensive stage lasted from the close of the World War to the double collapse of the Wrangel army in the Crimea, and the Polish invasion in the Ukraine. But in 1920 Soviet Russia passed to the offensive.

This offensive was, however, after an amazing forward sweep, decisively checked under the walls of Warsaw in a battle which had many resemblances to that of the First Marne in 1914. Following this defeat Red invasion ebbed swiftly, and the Treaty of Riga shortly put an end to the invasive phase of the Russian Revolution. So far this Revolution had followed in the footsteps of the French. It had made good its hold at home, it had launched a tremendous offensive abroad, but unlike the Revolutionary armies of 1795, the Red armies had been unable to carry a new doctrine victoriously over the Continent.

The Treaty of Riga marked the establishment of a state of balance between Russia and her enemies. All attempts to destroy the Red régime had failed, but similar failure had brought the Bolshevists back to their own frontiers. Both of the recent opponents still remained dominated by the fears born of struggle which had now terminated, but, in fact, neither was able or anxious to resume hostilities.

With the rise of Stalin to power, a third phase in Russian policy opened. Stalin perceived with admirable lucidity that a Twentieth Century Revolution, equipped with Fourteenth Century industrial and agricultural systems, could not hope to conquer a western world furnished with all the mechanical and technical equipment of a machine age. Therefore he undertook the colossal experiment of transforming his country, in fact, of imitating the methods of the capitalistic world in order to make possible a later attack. Nor in the policy of Stalin is it possible to overlook the example of Peter the Great.

In the nature of things, however, such an experiment condemned Russia to a period of passivity in the matter of foreign policy. Peace became the basic necessity of a country which was undertaking to reorganize its farm and factory alike. And tolerably friendly relations with the capitalistic nations were similarly inevitable, if the Soviet Union desired to draw from these both the machines and the men necessary for its own transformation.

For the time being, Red Russia had to fall into step with the capitalistic world to the extent of buying and selling, importing and exporting. And its need of peace was just as great as that of its recent and natural enemies. On the other hand, it was precisely as interested as ever in the maintenance of the Communist groups within the capitalistic countries, because these were destined to be invaluable allies when the moment to pass to the offensive again arrived.

Yet even in this detail of propaganda and incitation, the Soviet Union was faced with the necessity of observing a degree of moderation and consenting to a measure of sacrifice. What counted was the dominating need to create a domestic system of industrial and agricultural life. All else was temporarily subordinate and secondary. The World Revolution could wait on the Five Year Plan, but the Five Year Plan could not wait on anything.

The capitalistic world has been slow to appreciate this rather subtle evolution in Soviet policy, because it had been badly scared by previous Bolshevist policy, and remained rightly disturbed over the eventual consequences of Bolshevist purpose. Moreover, there was always the annoying detail of Communist agitation proceeding constantly although, in certain countries, with a discretion imposed by Soviet necessities.

It is clear, however, that for a period of a decade and perhaps longer, Russia has deliberately resigned not merely the purpose to make actual war, but, insofar as her governmental policy is concerned, to make trouble. In 1928, and succeeding years, Litvinoff appeared at Geneva and elsewhere, advocating disarmament, preaching economic non-aggression agreements, in fact, putting the peace makers of all other nations to shame by the extravagance of his pacific prescriptions.

The western world, which had long been alarmed over the prospect of Red Battalions crossing the Dniester, now became equally hysterical over the prospect of a Soviet economic offensive which was to flood a world, already three-quarters under water, with the products of factories and farms. This terror was, of course, purely fantastic, because, despite the fact that Russia's desperate need of funds to finance her foreign purchases incident to her industrialization programme, led to occasional dumping, the requirements of her population in food and manufactured articles were bound to absorb the production of her factories and her farms for a long time to come.

Only Germany was prompt to seize upon the opportunities of the Russian market and, at the same time, to attempt to exploit Russia politically. Thus for years Berlin was, on the one hand, ostentatiously aiding in the reorganization of the Red Army and, on the other, warning Europe against the peril of Bolshevism and the need of a strong Germany to resist it. This German manoeuvre was not in the least unwelcome to Soviet Russia precisely as long as relations with other capitalistic countries were difficult, if not impossible, and Germany could, herself, satisfy Soviet needs in materials and in credits.

The Bolshevists were not, however, in principle more friendly to a capitalistic Germany than to a bourgeois France. And the Nationalist elements in the Reich, who were most loudly celebrating the policy of the Eastern Orientation, were the most violent in their attacks upon the Communists within the German frontiers. Between the Russian and the German situation, too, there was a fundamental difference. The Reds were free agents, they could make political bargains where they chose. Thus it was far easier for the Soviet Union to exploit the Reich than for Germany to make use of the Reds.

Again, for the time being, Soviet interest lay patently not with Germany, which was trying to upset the existing order in Europe, but with France, which was the guarantor of the status quo, for although Moscow desired eventually to overturn the whole Continental system, it needed a peaceful Europe to insure that its own experiment should proceed undisturbed. And if political disorder produced social breakdown before Russia was ready, she would be unable to continue her experiment and would be obliged to renew her offensive with an equipment still inadequate to the task.

Thus, in the summer of 1931, Germany was profoundly disturbed by the unmistakable evidence of negotiations going forward between Paris and Moscow. The Franco-German struggle over the Anschluss had ended in the utter defeat of the Reich. German financial power had been wrecked and British had been compromised by the German collapse. Vienna and Budapest had reluctantly, but unavoidably, made their peace in Paris. The French system of alliances had taken on new force and the World Court had condemned the already abandoned Anschluss as illegal. If Paris could come to terms with Moscow, the French circle would be completed.

For Germany, a Franco-Russian non-aggression pact would, of course, have no fatal significance, but a similar pact between the Soviet Union and the Polish ally of France would spell the ruin of all the German hopes of an early suppression of the Polish Corridor. For in the back of all German minds is concealed a faith in an eventual Russian advance to Warsaw and a new partition of Poland, this time between two, and not three, powers. Thus, all Franco-Russian exchanges must be anxiously watched in Wilhelmstrasse.

The Franco-Russian conversations, which in the nature of things, could not be pushed to any immediate conclusion, disclosed in a striking fashion the return of Red Russia as a factor in European councils. It also illustrated again the fatal weakness,

which underlies all German efforts to achieve territorial revision. For a bankrupt Reich was in no
posture to outbid a country, whose national bank
was overflowing with gold, and the handicap was
the greater, because German need for a French loan
remained undiminished.

Even more interesting and important were these
Franco-Russian conversations and other similar epi-
sodes as evidences of the Soviet acceptance of the
necessity of a truce with western capitalistic states.
The logical assumption that the general prostration
of Europe, as a consequence of the economic depression, would inspire Russia to a fresh offensive
was demonstrated to be mistaken. Halfway through
the Five Year Plan Russia wanted peace quite as
much as Britain or France and saw her immediate
interests all bound up with those of her capitalistic
foes, and not with her communistic allies.

Napoleon III, in an unhappy moment, once proclaimed that his empire meant peace. Stalin, with
far greater accuracy, could affirm that, in its present
stage, the Red Revolution means tranquillity. True,
no one can say for how long. But, on the other
hand, all the outward evidences seem to suggest
that the time will be longer than is generally allowed. Looking to the longer future, nothing is less
likely than that a mighty Slav state, whether Soviet
or republican, will forever endure its present west-

ern frontiers. Nevertheless, while Moscow loves to raise goose-flesh in Bucharest by threats about Bessarabia, the Soviet leaders are not today thinking in terms of lost provinces or territorial revisions.

Red Russia has a great army, far more efficiently trained and vastly better equipped than that which in 1920 established two speed records, one in moving from the Niemen to the Vistula, and the other and better, in retiring from Warsaw to Grodno, but there is nothing to suggest that Moscow has any present intention to employ this army in a new offensive which would not bring any new security, and would inevitably upset all the rhythm of domestic re-organization.

In sum, then, the policy of Revolutionary Russia is, for the moment, constructive rather than destructive. It has need of immediate aid from a capitalistic system it hopes one day to abolish. Its necessities, too, drive it to seek some *modus vivendi* with a Paris which has become not alone the military, but the monetary capital of Europe. Moreover, Moscow can with reason conclude that the French political system is less likely to endure permanently, than that economic order which the German programme of European organization might establish in all of Central Europe.

Patently, Soviet policy is purely opportunistic, like Italian; and Bolshevism, like Fascism, is freed from all restraints arising from domestic political opposition. Red Russia is, however, also freed by its size and situation from many Italian limitations. Time runs against Italy everywhere, because on all sides, the present owners of provinces and colonies coveted by Rome, are consolidating their position. But if the Soviet Union can organize its colossal empire, its power will one day almost surpass imagination.

Unmistakably Moscow looks out upon the present crisis in the capitalistic world with unfeigned pleasure. For it, recent events have been an encouragement beyond calculation, but its present concern is not to force the pace. From a world it believes sinking, it is eager to snatch the last possible profit before passing again to the offensive. Status Quo and Revision policies are equally meaningless in Bolshevist calculations, understandings either with Berlin or Paris are of similarly transitory value. Undoubtedly the French and German calculations of exploiting the Red Revolution for national purposes, arouse equally intense amusement within the walls of the Kremlin.

The fact, however, remains, that having embarked upon his gigantic programme of domestic organizations, Stalin has, for the time being, given certain hostages to the capitalistic world. He is gambling that Europe cannot recover while Russia reorganizes. He is betting that the divisions between Status Quo and Revision peoples, the profound and seemingly impassable gap between the French and German purposes, in fact the civil war upon which capitalism itself has embarked, will serve his end, as a similar strife between the Greek cities prepared the way for Philip of Macedon.

Meanwhile, having whispered with Berlin, Stalin can talk with Paris. Since his enemy is playing his game in fact, why should he refuse for a little to play his enemy's to the greater glory and increased prestige of the Soviet Union?

Chapter Twenty-one

EUROPE, 1914-1932

VIEWED in the light of the policies of nations, it is clear that the resemblances between the Europe of 1914 and of today are at once impressive and significant. Pre-war Europe was a continent of coalitions—so is post-war Europe. The Triple Alliance which, by reason of its military power, dominated during the generation which preceded the World War, had its origin in the concern for security at the Rhine of the victor of 1870. The French system of alliances, which is supreme today, expresses the identical concern of the victor of 1918.

The guarantees France gives her Polish and Czech allies on the Vistula and the Danube are indistinguishable from those Germany gave her Austrian and Hungarian partners on the Save and the San. Because of the network of alliances and ententes which covered Europe in 1914, the crime of Serajevo could set half the world in flames. But because of the existence of a similar system in 1931, a proposal for Austro-German tariff union produced a political crisis felt with equal force in Paris and Berlin, Vienna and Warsaw, Budapest and Prague. And the financial repercussions of this crisis were disastrous in London, and disturbing even in New York.

In contemporary Europe, France has taken over the rôle of Germany in 1914. Similarly the Polish Corridor has replaced Alsace-Lorraine as the gravest cause of international discord. But concomitantly, Germany has adopted toward the Treaty of Versailles, that attitude which France maintained for more than forty years toward the Treaty of Frankfort.

In the old Europe the passions and purposes of the Balkan peoples were a constant peril to peace. But in the new, the Balkans begin at the Inn, and not at the Save, and the feuds dividing the peoples of the former Hapsburg Monarchy are not less violent and disruptive than those which separated the tribes dwelling in lands that had long been subject to the Sultan. Nor did the World War end the secular quarrels of the peoples of the old Balkans.

Similarly, while the World War brought no term to the hostility of France and Germany, the postwar years have seen the rapid development of rivalry between Italy and France and the transformation of the Alps into a frontier of fortification and friction recalling the Vosges before the war.

And as the Germany of 1914 was enclosed by allied enemies on the east and west, Italy now faces a similar coalition between France and Yugo-Slavia. From Rome, too, as in the old days from Berlin, proceeds familiar protest against a policy of "encirclement" and a purpose designed to deny a great people its rightful "place in the sun."

If, in spirit and national policies, the Europe of 1932 is identical with that of 1914, in physical circumstances the parallel is rather with the years following the Congress of Vienna. And by another ironical reversal of rôles, France, the insurgent of 1815, has become the conservator of 1914. Like the Holy Alliance, the French system of coalitions is designed exclusively to preserve a status quo established by force, and the prescription of peace of Poincaré and all other statesmen, who have ruled in Paris since the victory, has been identical with that of Metternich. Finally, as the permanence of the status quo created in 1815 depended solely upon the preservation of the overwhelming military power of the alliance which guaranteed it, that of 1919 rests upon a similar foundation.

Unlike the alliance of the conquerors of Napoleon, the contemporary coalition is not made up of the victors of the war—that partnership broke down in the Peace Conference—but only of France and those Succession States which find their security or

unity, established in the Paris Settlement, challenged by the purposes of the defeated nations. In
this respect, the French combination is far weaker
than the Holy Alliance, but in all else the parallel
is perfect, and, for the present, the power is
adequate.

Although they each endured for nearly half a
century, the territorial decisions of the Settlement
of Vienna and the Treaty of Frankfort were both
ultimately swept away because the peoples who
found their terms immediately intolerable, were
eventually able to challenge the power which sustained these systems. The spirit and purpose of the
German and Magyar races, today, is precisely that
of the nations which refused to accept the settlements of 1815 and 1871 as definitive. And as the
settlements of the past could only be revised by
war, no other method is discoverable today.

As a consequence, that simulacrum of peace
which exists on the Continent at the present hour
results uniquely from the exhaustion and helplessness of the unreconciled peoples. German efforts to
escape the bonds of Versailles, efforts which, in the
nature of things, could not extend to armed resistance, have been beaten down as swiftly and
decisively as Metternich stamped out the first
Italian efforts to upset the system of Vienna. But
the Italians continued even after Novara, and the

occupation of the Ruhr and the financial reprisals of the Anschluss episode have not broken German purpose, or shaken German determination.

In post-war Europe, a stupendous pantomime of peace has been acted at Geneva. The September session of the Assembly of the League of Nations has taken on something of the character of the Olympian Games in Ancient Greece. But before and after, the struggles of antiquity are reproduced in faithful detail. Foreign ministers, engaged in bitter controversy, return from the Swiss city, after a few brief days devoted to impressive but meaningless conversation, to resume their pursuit of irreconcilable purposes. And behind the facade of Geneva, the statesmanship of Europe continues to function in the traditional manner.

In sum, the spirit of peoples, the territorial issues which divide them, the policies which they severally pursue, are indistinguishable from the similar circumstances of 1914. The Europe of 1932 differs from the Europe of 1914 only in the fact that, while the purposes of nations remain irreconcilable, their power to pursue national policies to their logical conclusion, which is armed conflict, is temporarily lacking. But in all past time, this stage has proven transient.

A single profound change separates the Europe of yesterday from that of today. If the spirit and policies of peoples endure unmodified, and the nations face each other in the traditional temper, the position of the Continent, itself, in the world has undergone a complete transformation. As a consequence of the war, its old markets are lost, its former wealth is dissipated, the ancient bases of its power and prosperity have been dislocated, if not destroyed.

Thus the results of the World War seem to have placed Europe squarely face to face with the alternative of subordinating its political rivalries to its economic necessities, or of suffering collective ruin resulting alike from economic prostration and social upheaval. But, as yet, there is nothing to suggest that the democracies of Modern Europe are more capable of united action in the face of a common danger than were those of Ancient Greece in the presence of a common enemy. And no illustration of this fundamental anarchy could be more complete than that which was supplied during the great economic depression by the Anschluss episode.

Universally convinced that a new conflict would insure a disaster without limit, post-war mankind has easily adopted the conviction that such a war is at once impossible and unthinkable. But those who lived in the years between 1905 and 1914, when the last war was approaching with steady and unmistakable steps, must recall that the same conviction, and the same words, were equally common. Today, the purposes and policies which made the last war inescapable survive unmodified, and only the accommodation of seemingly irreconcilable policies can prevent that war, now pronounced impossible, from also becoming inevitable.

In 1914 war came, not because any people desired it, but because the policies which all peoples were pursuing and the objectives which they were seeking, could be realized only through victorious conflict. In 1932 the situation is unchanged. The Polish Corridor, the Anschluss, Hungaria Irredenta, all the territorial issues we have examined together, the policies of status quo and revision, expressing the will of peoples in the face of these territorial issues, are identical with the similar circumstances, which produced the universal conflict. And at the limit of every contemporary national policy is inescapable collision with another.

The generation which had reached maturity in 1904 will recall with clarity the series of incidents, which were the steps on the route to war. Tangier, Bosnia, Agadir, the long winter of 1913, when the peace of Europe literally turned on the disposition of Djacova, Prisrend and Dibra, because Russian and Austrian policies were in shock in the Balkans. Each crisis was more acute than the preceding, but the end of all crises was Serajevo. Each of these crises, too, marked a long step toward war, because while each left the resolution of peoples unmodified and their policies unchanged, it also produced a further exacerbation of national rancors.

But in the post-war Europe, the incidents have begun again. The occupation of the Ruhr, the far-sounding explosion of the Anschluss, both had their origin in the collision of national wills and purposes. And each for a moment, at least, lifted the curtain on which was painted the inspiring picture of a New Europe, to reveal the Old engaged in shifting scenery in preparation for a repetition of the traditional drama. One moment the world saw the statesmen of the Continent engaged in discussion of disarmament in Washington and of economic coöperation at Genoa, and, in the next, there passed before all eyes French troops and guns and tanks en route for Essen and Dusseldorf.

Eight years later the world saw Bruening and Curtius in Paris appealing for financial aid for their stricken country and receiving terms, which were those of a victor to a vanquished. A few weeks thereafter, Curtius was disclosed at Geneva making the same surrender in the Anschluss incident that was imposed upon Delcassé in the Moroccan, a quarter of a century before. And the humiliation for the German people in the post-war affair was not less than that for the French in 1905, nor was the comment of German nationalism different from that of French. But the drama which opened in Morocco ended at the Marne; or, more exactly, as the first act was the descent of William II at Tangier, the last was his flight to Holland. Nor can one fail to see, between the humiliating capitulation of Serbia after the Bosnian incident and the post-war surrender of Austria in the Anschluss affair, a parallel at once significant and striking.

Naturally the situation which exists in contemporary Europe, is not mistaken on the other side of the Atlantic. "The transition from a post-war to a pre-war era," was a famous British diplomat's description of the announcement from Berlin of the Austro-German tariff union. "A pause between crisis and catastrophe," was the phrase of the French Ambassador in Washington to define the Hoover Moratorium. "Let us go on a pilgrimage to the battlefield of Sadowa together," was the reported proposal of Benes to the French Minister in Prague, when the same Anschluss project was first disclosed.

Absence of armed conflict upon the European Continent, which in America is described as peace, results simply from the fact that peoples, who find the existing order intolerable are, by reason of economic exhaustion and financial weakness incapable of resorting to war, and their helplessness is further accentuated by the forcible disarmament of the Paris Settlement. But while it is clear that the present prostration may long continue, the spirit of the dissatisfied peoples gives to the existing situation the character of a postponement of hostilities, not of an authentic state of peace.

And, while this state of mind prevails, accommodation of territorial disputes and amendment of military restrictions, the basic demands of the dissatisfied peoples, are totally impossible. The truce of exhaustion may continue, but it is nevertheless clear that the prostration which today prohibits deliberate war may tomorrow provoke a conflict of despair. This danger can easily be exaggerated, but it cannot safely be ignored. For there are, at the present time, at least three possibilities of immediate conflict and they arise out of the purposes of National Socialism in Germany, the prospectus of Fascism in Italy and the fundamental programme of Bolshevism in Soviet Russia. Only the first constitutes an acute peril, but in all three countries, domestic conditions might impose a foreign adventure as the sole means of avoiding internal collapse.

It is, then, in the light of the temper of democracies, as disclosed at the Paris Peace Conference, and in the succeeding years; in the face of the territorial issues, and in the knowledge of the policies of peoples born of these territorial issues, that it is necessary to examine the experiments in peace of the post-war years, which is the final stage of our study.

PART FOUR

EXPERIMENTS IN PEACE

Chapter Twenty-two

PEACE BY CONFERENCE

FOR at least two centuries the English-speaking world has taken keenest delight in the description of the Irish as a race—

"Who fight like devils for conciliation
And hate each other for the love of God."

In the post-war years, however, no description could more exactly fit the attitude of peoples toward peace.

In theory, the task of organizing world peace is that of fashioning some "federation of mankind" in which national policies shall be voluntarily subordinated to international order. In practice, however, democracies have put the cart before the horse. They have invariably devised systems of world peace to accord with their national interests and then tried to impose these upon the rest of mankind.

America and Britain, secure behind their seas, have attempted, on the one hand, to end a state of anarchy in Europe unfortunate for their own prosperity and, on the other, to avoid entanglement in Continental quarrels which have no immediate importance for them. With the experience of the World War still fresh in their memories, both have been resolved to escape new involvements on old terms. All their proposals for peace, therefore, have been founded upon ethical and economic considerations. The sin and waste of war have occupied their peace propaganda. Arbitration, disarmament and the outlawry of war comprehend their proposals. Peace without responsibility is their major conception.

France and her allies have agreed in principle with all British and American proposals. Up to a point, their situation is identical. They are satisfied with their present circumstances and have no design upon the provinces or colonies of any nation. For them another war could only bring disaster without profit. They have, therefore, subscribed to all the pacts, shared in the creation of a World Court, led the way in arbitration agreements.

In one vital respect, however, the French situation is different from that of Britain or of the United States. The undisguised purpose of Germany and Hungary to recover territories lost through the peace treaties constitutes a menace to the Allies of France. In the face of this peril, France and her associates, Poland and the nations of the

Little Entente, ask that, in addition to the outlawry of war, there shall be some provision for force to keep the peace. Were the combined resources of mankind pledged to action against any aggression, neither Germany nor her former allies would venture to undertake the recovery of lost provinces by force. But British and American responsibility for European peace would be also established.

Germany presents a third prospectus. Like the rest of mankind, the German people desire peace, and for them the Anglo-Saxon programme is acceptable. But they insist that the basis of durable peace must be justice. And for them justice is lacking while the peace treaties endure unrevised. They frankly desire to acquire territories now belonging to other countries. But they defend this purpose by alleging that these territories were once theirs and were taken from them wrongfully and by violence.

It is plain, however, that these three prescriptions, peace without responsibility, peace with security and peace with revision, are irreconcilable. The British and American rests upon the principle of voluntary understanding, but today such understanding is lacking: the French and German formulas are mutually exclusive. As long as countries stick to their national conceptions, therefore, only deadlock can result. And so far in the post-war years the deadlock has continued unbroken.

In an attempt to reconcile these conflicting conceptions, however, democracies have had recourse to a new device. They have abandoned the older forms of private conversations between state departments and foreign offices and have employed international conferences instead. This represents a violent reaction against the old system due to the fact that peoples emerged from the World War convinced that the origin of that conflict could be traced to the secret processes of old-fashioned diplomacy.

Satisfied that publicity would prove a guarantee against a repetition of the tragic events of July, 1914, all peoples enthusiastically acclaimed Woodrow Wilson's slogan of "open covenants, openly arrived at." Yet with the exception of Locarno all purely political conferences have ended in failure. Washington, Genoa, the Coolidge Conference at Geneva, the London Naval Conference have supplied a continuous and monotonous record of high hopes similarly blasted.

Explanation of this failure has, however, been found not in the conference method itself but in lack of preparation or in the attitude of some nation. Yet, although lack of preparation has frequently been notorious, failure has invariably been due to neither circumstance but to the fact that all countries were equally unwilling to agree to those modifications of their own national policies, which alone would make international agreement possible.

In theory, an international conference is a meeting of minds to bring about an adjustment of international differences, but no meeting of minds is possible, when delegates have left their own minds at home. American representatives, who go abroad instructed to make no political agreements, French delegates, whose instructions permit them to make only political agreements, can arrive at no result. Any meeting of minds has, therefore, to take place before a conference, or not at all. The sole function of a conference must be to give effect to an agreement already reached. Otherwise delegates to such meetings are no more than travelling salesmen sent abroad to dispose of national policies. Their success will depend equally upon salesmanship and "sales resistance." And the agent who buys, as well as sells, will be discharged and his bargain repudiated, as happened to Woodrow Wilson.

At the London Naval Conference, for example, the American, British, French and Italian delegates were all inescapably bound in advance by the states of mind existing in their respective countries. They could not negotiate in the true sense of the word. They could only repeat in one another's presence day after day their respective national formulas.

When Stimson and Morrow attempted to break with their inhibition, which was "no political entanglements," the cable terminated their adventure. But it also doomed the Five Power Conference.

A three-power conference could have succeeded in London in 1930, although agreement between Britain and the United States had been impossible at Washington and Geneva, because after Geneva the British had changed their mind. They had perceived that in any competition in building with the United States the financial odds were hopelessly against them. They had, accordingly, decided that parity and friendship were better than enmity and a hopeless race. At the General Election of 1929, therefore, MacDonald had received a clear mandate from the British people to settle the American dispute and the conversations of Hoover and MacDonald at the Rapidan made agreement in conference certain. Japanese assent, too, was always to be obtained, for the question with Japan concerned tonnage and not policy.

On the other hand, a five-power conference was always hopeless, because Italy and France were at odds over the issue of parity and in the identical mood of Britain and the United States during the Washington and Geneva Conferences. It is true that all preparation was lacking in so far as the Latin countries were concerned, but the most meticulous regard for the feelings of both could not have changed the result. For Tardieu could not have remained in power if he had signed a treaty conceding parity to Italy unaccompanied by some guarantee pact accepted by the Anglo-Saxon nations. As for Grandi, he could not have returned to Rome, at all, if he had accepted a treaty without parity. Thus, once the London Conference had opened on a day of yellow fog, which was symbolical, it resolved itself into a dreary search for a formula to disguise a failure, which was inevitable.

Bad judgment, not poor preparation, invariably explains the failure of international conferences. And the bad judgment is disclosed in the convocation of conferences which are doomed to fail because there is no basis of agreement between the policies of nations. Since the United States was not prepared to sign a political pact, the French Note of December, 1929, advertised the certainty of failure at London. For the French announced that they would not agree to limitation without such a pact. Moreover, British and American newspaper correspondents in Rome and Paris reported the facts. The American and British embassies in Paris correctly informed their governments. But these governments were resolved upon a conference. And the same situation had existed before all other conferences which subsequently failed.

The explanation is invariably the same. For presidents and prime ministers alike, there is always a double temptation in the matter of an international conference. Such meetings distract domestic attention from troubles at home. Similarly, they insure a temporary rally of public opinion to the support of an administration actively engaged in foreign negotiation. Even the most unpopular of governments can calculate upon a truce in parochial political abuse for the duration of a foreign assembly, since it can always appeal for unity at home to promote success abroad. But that appeal is obviously foolish, in itself, because all other governments are making it simultaneously.

There is always, too, the much subtler temptation inherent in the opportunity provided by an international conference for a public man to address a world audience, to play a conspicuous rôle upon a larger stage, to appear, if only for a brief moment, as the spokesman of a world seeking peace. Thus international conferences have ended by creating an appetite for publicity, which no post-war statesman save Poincaré has been able completely to resist. Finally, public men always hope that, even if their conferences fail, they may still be praised for their effort, while the blame can be shifted to the representatives of another nation.

Yet it requires no profound examination of the consequences of the many unsuccessful conferences since 1919 to indicate how incalculable has been the harm resulting from the public disclosure of international rivalries at a time when the whole world was suffering both materially and psychologically from economic depression and political dispute. Conferences rashly summoned have led only to the exacerbation of national passions and international resentments. This fact explains the Geneva axiom that one disarmament conference is more disastrous for world peace than three battles in actual war. The same thought was disclosed in the prayer of a London clergyman after the Naval Conference—"Give to us peace in our time, oh Lord—peace without conference."

Nor is any detail of contemporary conferences more striking than the unfailing attempts of statesmen to conceal from their publics the truth concerning a meeting actually in progress. Their prestige being engaged, because they have prepared these publics for achievement, they are condemned to sustain the illusion of progress, to continue to hold out the promise of success and, in the end, in the face of a failure always inevitable, to claim a triumph which is promptly disclosed to have been lacking. Thus that secrecy and inveracity, which were the worst features of old-fashioned diplomacy have been adopted and even exaggerated by the new.

There is always, therefore, an element of basic untruth about international conferences. Publics perceive this promptly and have the uneasy feeling of being deceived by their own governments, as they are invariably suspicious of the superior skill of the representatives of other nations. Thus, as a consequence of successive failures they become cynical as to the possibility of any international understanding. As a means of attaining peace, accordingly, conferences have proven no more successful than were the methods of old-fashioned diplomacy in preventing war. And this failure results from the fact that they have been employed almost exclusively to help the political fortunes of administrations on the home front or to promote purely national policies abroad.

In the present state of public opinions in the world, only the certainty of success can justify summoning an international conference. And the evidence in the possession of governments is always adequate to foreshadow the result. Locarno, the single successful post-war conference, produced agreement, because, for almost a year before it was convoked, German, French and British statesmen,

aided by American ambassadors in Berlin and London, had been negotiating. When preliminary
agreement had been reached, Stresemann, Briand
and Chamberlain went to Locarno to settle minor
details and to sign. But all three knew in advance
that they were going to sign and all could count
upon the subsequent ratification of their agreement
by their respective parliaments.

Locarno treated the world to the welcome spectacle of French, British and German statesmen in
agreement for the first time since the outbreak of
the World War. As a result, there followed a
period of calm and reconstruction in Europe, which
lasted for four years. By contrast, the Washington
Conference opened a long stage of recrimination
between Britain and America and precipitated an
immediate explosion of Anti-French feeling in the
United States. Genoa intensified Franco-German
rancors and Anglo-French differences and thus insured the occupation of the Ruhr. After the Coolidge Conference, Anglo-American relations were
more unpleasant than at any time since the Civil
War. Following London, Franco-Italian rivalries
assumed an acute character and long disturbed
European tranquillity.

Nothing is, too, more impressive than the punish-
ment which is eventually exacted of public men
responsible for unsuccessful conferences. Both

Wilson and Clemenceau were the victims of Paris. Briand fell as a result of Washington. Lloyd George's fate was settled at Genoa. The fall of the Tory Government in England in 1929 was in no small measure the consequence of the Coolidge Conference. London was equally unfortunate for the domestic prestige of Hoover and of Mac-Donald.

Such condemnation is, too, thoroughly just, for responsibility for unsuccessful conferences rests squarely upon the shoulders of public men who insist upon convoking them. For these public men are able to discover the state of mind existing alike at home and abroad. And since at no international conference in the post-war era has there been any modification of policy on the part of any country, it is plain that disagreements existing before a meeting will only be accentuated during its sessions. Public opinion is, therefore, justified in indicting statesmen who, in the face of obvious facts, invite inevitable disaster.

When, as in the question of disarmament, the President of the United States insists upon an international conference, public opinion should ask him two questions: Has the United States changed its policy as to pacts? Have France and her allies modified their views as to security? If no reversal of policy has taken place in one case or the other, a disarmament conference must fail, because American and French delegates will go to Geneva committed in advance to irreconcilable theses, and an aroused public opinion in each country will make concession out of the question. However much delegates actually in presence may desire to make necessary compromises, they will remain the captives of their domestic Congress or parliament, which will themselves be the creatures of parochial public opinion. Thus the events of London will repeat themselves endlessly.

If the President of the United States desires a successful disarmament conference, his preparation for it must be an attempt to persuade his fellow-countrymen to modify their views upon foreign entanglements. If the Premier of France similarly desires achievement, he must try to persuade his fellow-citizens to change their ideas about security. These are the only useful preparations which can be made, and, lacking these, failure is assured. By contrast the notion that at a conference American delegates can convert French or French persuade American in the face of uncompromising national opinions is purely childish. Preparation for a successful foreign conference will always be made at home, not abroad.

Chapter Twenty-three

THE LEAGUE OF NATIONS

OF THE experiments in peace of the post-war world, the League of Nations is beyond question the most ambitious and the most important. In a measure, at least, it represents the single solution Democracy has as yet been able to find for the most serious of all its problems. If, too, the experiment has so far failed, it still continues, and no substitute for the League has even been suggested. The world hope for peace remains centered in Geneva, and, in addition, the League has already taken its place as a necessary and permanent instrument of international coöperation.

The evident success of the Geneva institution in a limited sphere, and the usefulness which it plainly possesses, cannot, however, distract attention from the fact that it has so far failed to realize the major hope of mankind at the moment of its creation. And that hope was patently for an international institution, which would permit the organization of world peace and the removal of the causes and dangers of new conflict. Thoreau wrote that man sets out in life to construct a palace and ends by building a woodshed, but while the League is in the process of achieving its palace, it remains as far as ever from providing a shelter for peace.

The explanation of the failure of Geneva is amply disclosed in the brief history of the League itself. In its very origin it did not represent a general conception, nor a plan in which the ideas of all nations had fused into a single programme; on the contrary, it was purely and simply an Anglo-Saxon proposal. And if, in the actual draft of the Covenant, the British hand was more active than the American, the decisive impulse and the dominating idea were those of the American President.

For Wilson, the Paris Conference had a two-fold task: to make a just peace and to fashion an institution in which all people, in full and equal coöperation, could assure the perpetuation of that peace. And, in the mind of the American President, his Fourteen Points supplied a platform on which just and equitable re-organization of Europe was possible, while the League insured the continuation of an understanding to be established by the peace treaties.

The view of the European peoples, who constituted the Allied and Associated Powers, was quite different. To be sure, British and American opinions were readily harmonized, but between Anglo-Saxon and Continental conceptions, there was no common ground. The victorious and Succession states not only demanded satisfaction for their territorial claims, but military guarantees for their future security, as well. When, too, the Germans came to Versailles, Wilson promptly discovered that they were as unwilling to accept the programme of the Fourteen Points on the Vistula as the French on the Rhine.

Born in this chaos of Paris, the League of Nations was laid on the door-step of Europe, by the retreating America, to be adopted and reared in accordance with European tradition. The history of the League, during its brief existence, naturally falls into three periods: that of organization from 1920 to 1925, that of temporary success, from 1926 to 1929, and that of crisis and decline from 1929 to the present hour.

Between 1920 and 1925, the rôle of the League was insignificant and its international activities slight. The great events, of which the occupation of the Ruhr was the most important and the bombardment of Corfu the most sensational, proceeded without reference to the League or regard for Geneva. All the friends of the League waited, hopefully at first, and then with growing disappointment, for the return of the United States.

Meantime, Germany being excluded, and official Britain little interested, the actual organization of the League was undertaken by representatives of France, of the Succession States and of the neutrals of the World War. And in the absence of the Anglo-Saxon powers and of the enemy states, the question of security was always in the foreground.

After four years the League formula of security was presented to the Assembly of 1924 in the presence of the Labor Prime Minister of Britain and the President of the French Council, who was a Radical. This formula, which was the most significant detail of the once famous Protocol, reinforced the Covenant of the League by a more specific undertaking, on the part of the member nations, to take action to restrain and to coerce any nation guilty of aggression. It thus placed at the disposal of the League the collective resources of member nations for action against any individual state violating the pledge of the Covenant, and held guilty of such violation by the Council of the League itself.

Acceptance of the Protocol by the nations belonging to the League would automatically have made the Geneva body the guarantor of all the terms of the peace treaties, because, manifestly, no revision of these treaties was possible except with the consent of the nations concerned. Thus, in effect,

the Protocol would have accomplished the purpose
which had been expressed by the French in the
Paris Conference, first, in the proposal of Léon
Bourgeois to provide the League with a general
staff, and second, in Clemenceau's guarantee treaty,
signed by Wilson and Lloyd George, but later rejected by the American Senate.

Against this Protocol, MacDonald spoke ear-
nestly, although he later signed it. But the Tory
Cabinet which soon replaced Labor declined to rat-
ify it. This action, which MacDonald had forecast,
indicated that the British people were as little willing, through the Protocol, to engage their blood
and treasure to maintain the peace treaties as the
Americans had been to undertake similar obligations in the Covenant. Once again, the utter diver-
gence between Anglo-Saxon and Continental views
was disclosed.

With the beginning of the discussions which in
1925 led to the making of the Locarno Pacts, a new
stage opened in Geneva. French statesmanship,
guided by Briand, and encouraged by Britain, abandoned the effort to base security solely upon the
League and sought to arrive at direct agreement
with Germany. And the adoption of the Pacts of
Locarno was followed the next year by the admis-
sion of Germany to the League.

During the next three years, Briand, Stresemann

and Chamberlain made Geneva the centre of a work of international coöperation in which Britain, France and Germany participated on a footing of equality. This was the great period in League history. Its assemblies, which had long been neglected, suddenly became brilliant sessions attended by the prime ministers and foreign ministers of the whole Continent. The spirit of Locarno continued to influence Franco-German relations. The Ruhr, and then the Rhineland, were evacuated. The reparations clauses of the Treaty of Versailles, revised in 1924 by the Dawes Plan, were again amended in 1929 by the Young Plan. Economic coöperation between France and Germany through cartels gave the further impression of veritable reconciliation. Geneva almost in an hour took on the semblance of a world capital.

With the death of Stresemann, however, the change was swift and far-reaching. The sun of Locarno disappeared behind the clouds of a gathering Nationalist storm in the Reich. The German people, who had hoped, by entering the League, to escape from all reparations and recover their eastern frontiers, were now disappointed by the postponement of their dreams and resumed their attack alike upon the financial, military and territorial provisions of the Treaty of Versailles. The French, taking alarm at the new challenge, became again concerned about their security. And their Polish and Czech allies shared their apprehension. Briefly, Europe relapsed to the atmosphere of the period of the occupation of the Ruhr.

Inevitably, this recrudescence of old quarrels was echoed in the sessions of the League itself. The clash between French and German policies in the matter of disarmament all but disrupted the work of the Preliminary Arms Conference. The selection of a chairman for the long delayed definitive meeting divided the Council, with Germany supporting Arthur Henderson, the British Foreign Secretary, and France urging Benes, the Czech Foreign Minister. The question of the treatment of her German minority by Poland provided Curtius with an admirable basis for attack upon Zaleski.

Thus the League, which in Wilson's dream was to be the meeting-place of peoples resolved in concert to maintain and extend European peace and coöperation, became the battle-ground of national policies and a mirror of Continental anarchy. European statesmen manœuvred to obtain the favors of South American delegates, and even of Chinese, whose votes acquired importance in the Council and in the World Court. And, inescapably, the very prescriptions of peace, which were to bring international tranquillity, became the issues of battle between quarrelling nations and groups of nations.

Disarmament projects were considered, not on their merits, but in the light of the political associations of the nations presenting them; economic proposals were rejected without consideration by one foreign minister seeking to diminish the prestige of another. Where, in pre-war Europe, international disagreements had been carried on by the deliberate and secret methods of old-fashioned diplomacy, they were now conducted by statesmen in public sessions in the League of Nations halls, and the evidence of irreconcilable differences was transmitted by the eye-witnesses of the press with a speed and vigor which recalled the accounts of prize fights reported by rounds. The day's proceedings were summarized as a victory for France, a humiliation for Germany, a defeat for Great Britain, by the war-correspondents of peace.

As a consequence dimly, at first, but with ever-growing clarity, peoples everywhere began to realize that the League of Nations was not a guarantee of peace. They saw the disputes over the Polish Corridor, the Anschluss, Franco-Italian naval parity growing daily more acute. They recognized that the Kellogg Pact, like the Covenant of the League, constituted no insurance against future conflict. They comprehended that, despite all the interminable disarmament conferences, nations were again arming, and that statesmen who occasionally embraced at Geneva invariably continued to quarrel elsewhere. In their eyes, the League came more and more to appear a façade of pretense behind which the old realities remained.

Disappointment was, too, accentuated, when the great economic crisis disclosed Geneva as little effective in the service of world prosperity as of international peace. Briand's grandiose prospectus of Pan-Europe was outlined against the stark reality of a universal and growing prostration. Finally, the Austro-German plan for tariff union precipitated a crisis which instantly recalled the worst of the prewar clashes. In the face of facts which were not longer to be disguised, the still uninterrupted flow of League professions angered a public it no longer impressed.

A little more than a decade after the launching of the experiment, therefore, the League is in full crisis. The disillusionment which followed the Paris Conference is now repeated after each session of the League. But, once more, peoples who are acutely aware of the fact of failure remain totally oblivious to the causes. Thus, while the Anglo-Saxon powers continue at Geneva to press for disarmament, the Status Quo nations similarly clamor for security, and the Revision countries still demand territorial changes.

Yet it is unmistakable that the League cannot apply all of these mutually exclusive programmes at one time, or any one of them at all, save by unanimous consent. The League can have no power other than that which may be delegated to it by member nations. But no nation has yet consented to any delegation. The United States refused to join because of the nightmare of the superstate. The British Parliament rejected the Protocol because of fear that it might put a foreign mortgage upon its fleet and army. France places its right to security, and Germany, its claim to revision, above all present or prospective League authority.

Thus, in reality, the fate which has now overtaken the League, is identical with that which ultimately destroyed the Concert of Europe. From the Congress of Berlin to the Assassination of Serajevo, the great powers, acting together, brought Europe through innumerable crises without conflict. As late as the Conference of Algeciras in 1905, a general war over Morocco was avoided, as similar conflict over Turkey had been prevented a generation before. Even in 1913, a conference of ambassadors liquidated the Balkan Conflicts peacefully.

But, in 1914, the great powers had become hopelessly divided into rival alliances. As a consequence, no basis of agreement was discoverable in the tense and tragic days, which briefly preceded the catastrophe. Russia and Austria stood rigidly to their respective solutions. France and Germany supported their allies faithfully. Britain, despite the frantic efforts of Sir Edward Grey, could invent no compromise. Today, at Geneva, although the crisis is chronic, and not acute, the situation is identical. As the Concert of Europe dissolved into quarrelling coalitions, the League of Nations has degenerated into irreconcilable groups of countries. And the rôle of Britain is as futile as in 1914.

Today, statesmen of all countries go to Geneva to impose national views. And their publics watch them from afar prepared to dismiss them if they consent to any modification or surrender of national purposes. When, however, deadlock inevitably arrives, each people first blames another nation, and eventually the League itself. Each believes that Geneva is an instrument to give international effect to its own national policies. But the notion of the League of Nations imposing an alien prescription upon themselves is utterly repugnant, and wholly intolerable for all peoples.

In practice, therefore, the attitude of peoples toward the League of Nations is completely comprehended in the famous nursery rhyme—

"Mother, may I go out to swim?
Yes, my darling daughter,
Hang your clothes on a hickory limb,
But don't go near the water."

The League is forbidden, under its constitution, to undertake the solution of any of the great problems which are disturbing the peace of contemporary Europe, because it can act only by unanimous consent. Nevertheless, it is everywhere condemned for failing to provide the world with a viable system of order. And, as the danger of new conflict visibly expands, the prestige of the League inevitably contracts. The paradox of a world institution to prevent war, and of issues which must eventually produce war, developing side by side, is necessarily fatal.

What is true of the League is also true of its dependent parts, such as the World Court. They, too, are rigidly restricted in their fields of activity. Moreover, the advisory opinion handed down by the Hague Tribunal in the case of the Austro-German tariff union gravely impaired the standing of the court before the world, because it disclosed the judges following the notorious example of the Supreme Court of the United States in the Hayes-Tilden case and dividing in accordance with the partisan interests of the countries to which they belonged. France, Poland and Rumania were on one side, Germany on the other.

Some Americans and many Europeans have laid great stress upon the absence of the United States from Geneva and have sought to explain the present failure of the League as due to this circumstance. But while it is possible to dismiss with utmost contempt practically all of the arguments which have been urged against American membership, none of the champions of American entrance have proposed any concrete contribution that the United States could make in the present crisis at Geneva.

In 1917, the United States entered the World War and in the eyes of the American President that intervention was designed to bring the world to a just and enduring peace. But the single practical result of American participation in the war was to enable one group of Continental powers to defeat another and to impose its terms upon the defeated coalition. The vanquished, in their turn, have ever since declined to accept these terms as definitive. Thus the European situation, despite a present state of nominal peace, is actually identical with that which existed when America entered the war.

As the situation now stands, the United States, as a member of the League of Nations, could support the Status Quo powers in their attempt to impose the terms of the peace treaties, or Germany and the other Revision states in their endeavor to compel treaty modifications. But in both cases, it would simply be joining in a European dispute and, in either instance, the objective sought would involve the use of American force. Nor is there discoverable any third line of action.

It is true that there exists on this side of the Atlantic the purely fantastic idea that, in some undescribed manner, American idealism can show Europe the way to reform. But the Polish Corridor is today a European monument to American idealism, and while many believe Wilson's decision in this case was just, none will argue that it has contributed to peace. In practice, too, American participation in the various disarmament conferences has not been accompanied by concrete contribution. On the contrary, nothing has happened save that one more discordant opinion has been voiced contentiously at Geneva.

In or out of the League, too, it is evident that the American people will not abandon the conviction, which is in the very depth of their national soul, that peace cannot be made by force, nor maintained by coercion. It is perfectly true that this conviction is born of purely American experience and circumstance, and that Continental European peoples with a different history and a dissimilar geographical situation have other views. But those Europeans who are eager to have America join the League are influenced in this desire solely by the belief that America at Geneva would support their respective national policies. Conversely, the Americans who urge membership have no other thought than that, once formally established in the League, American idealism would show the way to peace.

In sum, the present failure of the League arises uniquely from the fact that it is an international institution in the hands of peoples who can only think and act nationally. As a consequence, each country seeks to employ the machinery of the League to its own ends. Because the treaties of the Paris Settlement are the law of Europe, and cannot be changed save by violence, the Status Quo powers, led by France, have been able to make Geneva a useful instrument to serve their purposes. By contrast, French predominance in the League has, on the one hand, reduced British enthusiasm for the Geneva organization and, on the other, evoked German threats to abandon it altogether. And the French, although their influence is patently predominant, are still manifestly unsatisfied. Thus, in the present attitude of peoples, the true explanation of the failure of the League is discoverable.

For the dozen years of its existence, League champions have urged, not without reason, that the very vastness of the undertaking required patience and sympathy for the Geneva institution. Nevertheless, it is impossible to blink the fact that in recent years all progress has been arrested, and the patience of the masses tends to become exhausted. Since, too, in the nature of things, only moral authority is available for the League, it is manifest that a decline in confidence can prove fatal. And that decline is obviously taking place.

The tragedy disclosed in the spectacle of democracies engaged in the deliberate sabotage of the single instrument of international coöperation in existence is, too, unmistakable. Nor is it lessened by the obvious fact that the League of Nations is the only answer Democracy has yet discovered to the ever-present challenge of Red internationalism. And, if Geneva ultimately fail, all the profit will be with Moscow.

Chapter Twenty-four

THE KELLOGG PACT

THE Kellogg Pact is, beyond all else, interesting and important as the most perfect expression of the American conception of a system of world peace yet discovered. The Covenant of the League of Nations was a joint product of British and American thought. By contrast, the Kellogg Pact is pure United States. Nor does subsequent adoption by a French Foreign Minister, or later extension to include all nations, mar its fundamental spirit.

Of itself, the Kellogg Pact undertakes to do two things: to make war illegal, and to pledge nations who renounce war as an instrument of policy to settle their disputes by arbitration. In its essence, it amounts to precisely the same formal pledge, signed by nations, that in ancient days advocates of Temperance, as it was then called, invited drunkards to take, in renunciation of the use of alcohol.

At the basis of this contract, too, is the ineradicable American conviction that European peoples are addicted to war, as individuals to the excessive use of liquor. Thus, in spirit and in text, the Kellogg Pact is the Eighteenth Amendment of international law. The single, but all-important distinction between the Prohibition programme and that of the Kellogg Pact lies in the fact that in the latter neither the power nor the means to enforce the law against war is provided. And as the Eighteenth Amendment, in practice, is not invoked to prevent the use of alcohol as medicine, the Kellogg Pact, too, permits the resort to war in self-defense.

In reality, two quite distinct conceptions are fused in the Kellogg Pact, the juridical and the pacifistic. Lawyers celebrate the document because, for the first time, war is established as illegal in international law. Pacifists hail it because, similarly for the first time, war is abolished by proclamation. Nevertheless, lawyers are faced by the anomaly of a law which is unenforceable, while pacifists are condemned to note that preparations for conflict continue everywhere undiminished.

For Americans, too, the Kellogg Pact presents a certain incongruity. Had it been in force in 1777, their Revolution would have failed. That failure, of course, would not have been due to any proscription of the right of rebellion, but to the fact that the intervention of France would have been rendered impossible. Precisely in the same way, the several struggles of the Greeks, Belgians, Italians

and of the Balkan peoples for independence must
have come to nothing, because those interventions
by other nations which crowned them with success,
would have been prohibited.

The Declaration of Independence and the American Constitution being what they are, however, it
is clear that the people of the United States can
justify the implications of the Kellogg Pact only on
the assumption that, in the present fortunate age,
all peoples have at last attained liberty and unity:
or, by contrast, that some means other than war has
been discovered, by which these blessings may be
acquired. Otherwise the Kellogg Pact would condemn peoples now in chains to suffer eternally, save
as they, unlike the American Colonists, are able to
free themselves unaided.

In reality, however, no such situation exists. Lay-
ing aside all the territorial disputes of Central Europe, there is the case of the great Ukrainian people.
Today this race numbering above forty millions is
partitioned between three nations, as Poland was
before 1919. Czecho-Slovakia, Poland and Soviet
Russia each contain Ruthenian populations. And in
the post-war years the Ukrainians have fought un-
successfully, both against the Poles and the Bolshevists. Their present hope of liberty rests uniquely
upon the possibility of war between Russia and

some great power, as Italian hopes were once based upon an Austro-French conflict.

The fundamental weakness of the Kellogg Pact arises from the attempt to make war a crime, although no people is prepared to consider as criminal the struggles by which it acquired independence and unity, or renounce the blessings thus acquired. It expresses an American conviction, based exclusively upon American circumstances, that, although war was once justifiable, it has now become unnecessary, since all the possible purposes of just war have been realized. Instinct in the American state of mind is the belief that civilization has now progressed beyond the stage of armed conflict. And along with this belief goes the perception of the incalculable destruction which modern war involves.

Nevertheless, it is instantly evident that no people is now prepared to abandon its hope of acquiring independence or unity either because the satisfied peoples unite to pronounce conflict criminal or because the evidence of the World War discloses that the consequences of modern war are catastrophic. The Kellogg Pact reposes upon the assumption that the danger of war arises uniquely from the evil passions of peoples and their similarly immoral ambitions. But the slightest examination of the realities of the European situation discloses that, in the main, the graver perils arise from the pursuit by peoples of irreconcilable aspirations for national unity and security indistinguishable from those of the American and British nations which have, to be sure, been fulfilled.

The Kellogg Pact would, therefore, be a perfect instrument, when applied to a world actually at peace and, for example, to the relations between the United States and Canada. But it can have no practical application to Continental relations as illustrated by Polish-German circumstances. And, for the United States and Canada, its value would be slight, because the danger of war is wholly non-existent.

Accepted literally, the Kellogg Pact would destroy the last remaining hope of the German, Hungarian and Bulgarian peoples to recover their national unity. It would condemn the Ukrainian race to perpetual servitude. In the hands of the Holy Alliance after 1815, it would have been an instrument of oppression of incalculable value. But, of course, none of the partitioned peoples of present-day Europe will renounce its hopes of national resurrection, and therefore, while all signed, the effect was precisely *nil*. Everything proceeded exactly as before. And, although the Pact was executed in 1929, the European situation has continued to worsen ever since.

Most significant of all, too, was the fact that the ink was barely dried upon the parchment, when there came from Paris the proposal that the Kellogg Pact should be provided with teeth. And of course Europe is always striving to amend the dentistry of American idealistic programmes. At the Paris Conference, it was the matter of providing a general staff for the League of Nations. At Geneva, it was the question of the Protocol. At the London Naval Conference, it was the case of a consultative pact to precede the limitation of armaments.

If the Kellogg Pact were, in fact, more than a pious resolution, no teeth would be required. Once, however, it were furnished, even with the false teeth of a consultative pact, as is frequently urged, it would become a new weapon in the armory of the Status Quo powers, and in the eyes of the Revision nations, would appear a fresh instrument of oppression. It would, in effect, not only make criminals of all peoples who sought to attain liberty and unity by the sole means available, but also provide means for punishing them.

The Kellogg Pact does bar the way to the only kind of war of which the American people can, themselves, conceive, namely a war of aggression deliberately provoked to promote national aggrandisement. But it just as clearly closes the door to wars waged for objectives which every people, beginning with the American, have held—and continue to hold—noble and above reproach. And it is precisely at this point that the great mass of American propaganda for peace, and the vast bulk of the activities of American peace societies, break down. They undertake to exorcise a devil, which does not exist, and ignore a danger, which is real.

No error of all of those common to American appraisals of European conditions is so complete as that which, on the basis of American circumstances, mistakes the European status quo for a state of actual peace, and assumes the acceptance of the existing situation by all right-minded and intelligent men and women of every Continental country as the point of departure for the attempt to abolish war. In effect, this amounts to an attempt to instruct Europeans in the way to preserve a state of peace enjoyed only by Americans and Britons.

To this colossal misapprehension, too, was due that astounding post-war phenomenon, when the peoples of a continent whose richest cities were in ruins, whose fairest provinces had been laid waste, whose homes, almost without exception, were in mourning, were condemned to submit to endless exhortations designed to convince them that war was a curse and peace a blessing. All of these exhortations, too, not only came from a people dwelling on the safe side of the Atlantic, but were also based upon the preposterous assumption that immunity from misery, due exclusively to geographical circumstances, was the direct consequence of a finer morality and of a higher intelligence.

In point of fact, however, all citizens of any one of the belligerent countries knew, from direct experience, immeasurably more about the horrors of war than any resident of the United States who remained at home during the great struggle. And at least there is rudimentary intelligence enough amongst all European peoples to perceive that the rewards of peace are more attractive than the penalties of strife. By contrast, what portion of the far famed American passion for peace would survive life-sentence to the conditions of German, Hungarian, or Bulgarian minorities in the Corridor, on the Island of Schutt, or in Macedonia? Or a return to the circumstances from which the Pole, the Czech and the Southern Slav have recently escaped?

Between the savages who, ignorant of sanitation and science, see in disease the visible manifestation of the presence of malevolent spirits, and those Americans who, ignorant of the primary facts of the European Continent, explain the dangers of European conflict by an hagiology all their own, peopled by the horrendous demons of militarism, imperialism and chauvinism, the analogy is complete. And, in fact, although the great mass of the

American people have long ago abandoned incantation as a method of curing disease, a majority are still convinced of its efficacy in preventing war.

As a consequence, all American prescriptions for peace, the Covenant of the League, the Kellogg Pact, the Washington proposals for disarmament, since they proceed from the same fundamental misinterpretation of European facts, are precisely as appropriate to Continental problems as furs generously offered to Equatorial tribes. And Continental peoples, for their part, invariably follow the illuminating example of the Cuban natives who, having received from Lord Timothy Dexter of Newburyport, a consignment of warming pans, knocked off the covers and used them to dip molasses. In the same manner, the French would furnish the Kellogg Pact with teeth and use it to perpetuate the Treaty of Versailles.

Chapter Twenty-five

DISARMAMENT

No PROBLEM of the post-war world has been attacked more frequently or with less success than that of disarmament. Uniform failure has not, however, been due, as is so generally believed, to any lack of perception on the part of peoples of the waste and danger of military establishments maintained on the scale of Continental Europe. On the contrary, the burdens upon the taxpayer, the sacrifice demanded of the youth of countries which employ the conscript system, the inevitable implications of the vast armies themselves, these circumstances have everywhere been perceived with equal clarity.

Failure of all efforts to bring about an international adjustment of the problem of armaments has been due primarily to the fact, little perceived in Anglo-Saxon countries, that armaments are but a subordinate detail in the far larger question of peace. In reality, armies and navies alike are only the means by which national policies are carried out. Thus, all reduction of military and naval forces waits upon a prior adjustment of the policies of nations. And since, up to the present time, the policies of Continental peoples remain irreconcilable, disarmament conferences have led promptly and fatally to a collision of these policies.

British and American publics have wholly failed to perceive the political implications. For them, the way to disarm is to disarm. The invariable practice of European nations of complicating the question of the size of armies and the number of ships by raising all sorts of issues concerning the peace treaties and the territorial issues, has been at once inexplicable and intolerable to peoples who continue to view the question of disarmament as a simple matter of economics and of ethics.

Anglo-Saxon conceptions are, however, a curious mixture of hypocrisy and blindness. The hypocrisy is disclosed in the fact that for themselves both Great Britain and the United States claim complete and overwhelming naval supremacy in those waters which are vital to them. No Continental state possesses, through its army, any such measure of security as belongs to Britain or to the United States as a consequence of its naval establishment. And, although both nations discuss disarmament, neither has any intention of modifying, in the smallest degree, the relative superiority which it maintains.

The blindness arises from the fact that, since there is no collision between the policies of the British and American peoples, no political adjustment has been necessary in advance of the naval agreements. On the other hand, both peoples conveniently ignore the fact that, before the agreements of the Washington Conference were made with Japan, a long and difficult political negotiation was necessary. And the end of this negotiation was the consent on the part of America and England alike, to refrain from further fortification of a vast area, which extends from the Aleutian Islands to the Dutch East Indies, and includes the Philippines and Guam.

In a word, before any adjustment of naval strength between the Anglo-Saxon powers and the Japanese was possible, Japanese prescriptions as to security had to be met completely. When these were met, the three great naval powers could adjust their respective naval establishments. The terms of the adjustment, too, allotted absolute supremacy to each in its domestic waters and precluded any possibility of a successful offensive by any in the vital areas of either of the others. At bottom, this adjustment was only possible, however, because the policies of the three countries were not opposed.

So far, the limit of success of all armament regulation since the war has been this Anglo-American-

Japanese compact originally framed in Washington in 1922 and conditionally extended at London in 1930. Failure to extend this agreement definitively had its origin in the dispute between France and Italy over the question of parity. France, as the second colonial power of the world, with a vast empire in Africa, and a considerable estate in Asia, has demanded for herself the rank of a first class naval power.

Her naval establishment, too, is based upon a national policy, which aims at maintaining her lines of communication with her Mediterranean colonies of Algeria, Tunis and Morocco, menaced by the Italian fleet, and her Channel and Atlantic lanes, vulnerable to attack by the small but highly efficient German navy. The obvious possibility of an eventual Italo-German alliance, therefore, dictates to France the necessity of a two-power standard.

Italy, for her part, since it is a matter of life or death for her to keep open the waterways by which food and raw materials reach her peninsula, and, in addition, since her population is superior to that of Continental France, demands parity with her neighbor beyond the Alps. Unmistakable questions of prestige and jealousy enter into the Franco-Italian question, but, at bottom, French demand for a two-power standard in the face of Italy and Germany is on all fours with the British two-power standard policy which amounts to a tradition, while the Italian demand for parity with France parallels the American insistence upon equality with Britain.

Neither the French nor the Italians in their calculations are concerned with British, American, or Japanese naval establishments. No political questions exist, and for them, for all practical purposes, the navies of these powers function on different planes. On the other hand, the British are immediately concerned with French and Italian sea strength, because the most important lane of British imperial communications passes through the Mediterranean. Britain, therefore, insists upon a fleet equal to the combined strength of France and Italy.

The United States, uninterested in Franco-Italian fleets, but resolved upon parity with Britain, finds itself faced with the fact that the size of its own navy must be based upon the combined strength of the French and Italian. Thus it becomes a matter of concern for Washington to persuade the Latin powers to keep their fleets at a low tonnage. Only in this way can any limit be put upon American naval expenditure. At this point, then, the United States becomes involved in a European political problem.

The Italians are quite ready, on the basis of parity with France, to set their tonnage low, because theirs is a poor country. And, in reality, their only chance of attaining parity with France, save in battleships, which was agreed upon at Washington but never accomplished in fact, lies in joining the Anglo-Saxon states in exerting pressure upon France. For France has the money to maintain a fleet which Italy cannot rival.

On the other hand, the French, financially quite able to maintain a two-power standard, are only willing to abandon this course, if the danger, against which it is constructed, is exorcised. And the sole means of exorcising it is through some form of Mediterranean Locarno, which would insure to the French the support of the Anglo-Saxon fleets, provided, after they had conceded Italian parity to satisfy American desires for cheap equality with Britain, they were assailed by a German-Italian coalition.

It was at this point that the London Naval Conference broke down, because the Hoover Administration, exactly informed as to the temper of Congress, was unwilling to approve of any form of political agreement, even a consultative pact. Thus Anglo-American-Japanese adjustments made at London were conditional. Britain reserved the right to exceed the Three Power Treaty limits, if such action were necessary in order to maintain the two-power standard in the face of the two Latin countries. Washington and London thereafter endeavored to bring about an agreement between Paris and Rome, but long failed with the result that the naval undertakings of London had a purely provisional character.

It is manifest, however, that no solution of the naval question is even conceivable until the political questions are disposed of. France will not subordinate her security, menaced by the aims of two nations, pursuing policies frankly contrary to her own, to any Anglo-Saxon programme. Thus, adjustment waits upon a removal of the political differences between France and Italy, on the one hand, and France and Germany, on the other, or upon an acceptance by the Anglo-Saxon nations of the French demand for some form of guarantee.

The question of the reduction or limitation of land armaments is much more complicated, but similarly turns upon political consideration. Here, too, the break between Anglo-Saxon and Continental conceptions is complete. Neither the British nor the American army is considerable or above the irreducible minimum consonant with national needs. Nor in American or British eyes is the army the vital element in national defense. By contrast, Continental armies are not only large, but constitute the chief factor in assuring the security of the nations which maintain them. Only Germany, and the other states which were defeated in the World

War are rigidly limited by treaty to forces which bear no relation to national conceptions of security.

The French army, like the navy, is based upon possible combination of Germany and Italy. It must, therefore, be strong enough to defend the frontiers of the Rhine and the Alps and, in addition, to protect the various colonies. In her calculations, France can and does take into consideration the aid that would come from her Czech and Polish allies in the face of Germany and from her Yugo-Slav ally in the case of Italy. But Poland is, in turn, faced by a Russian danger, Czecho-Slovakia by a Hungarian, and Yugo-Slavia by a Bulgarian.

All this vast and intricate system of armaments is founded upon very precise mathematical calculations. The technical estimates of the probable dangers are expressed in terms of divisions, guns, air squadrons and tanks. The general staff plans of all the armed countries are based upon the existing strength, and the plans of operation to be employed after mobilization and concentration are similarly prepared. Thus, mere rough and ready reduction would upset the whole mechanism. And it is worth recalling again that the blunder of Moltke in sending two army corps to East Prussia after the Battle of the Frontiers led directly to the fatal defeat of the Marne.

Accordingly, when the Anglo-Saxon powers ap-

proach France and her allies, asking for a reduction
of land armaments, they are confronted at once by
very practical questions. Further reduction of the
armies of Germany, Austria and Hungary is out
of the question, since they were fixed by the treaties
at a level which left them barely adequate for domestic police. Reduction of the armies of France
and her allies would therefore automatically diminish their protection in the face of dangers which
would not be proportionately scaled down.

France and her allies say quite simply that reduction of their land armaments is out of the question
save as such reduction is balanced by some new and
equal guarantee of security. That guarantee they
all see in the agreement of the Anglo-Saxon powers
to support them against any unprovoked attack.
And, since they, themselves, contemplate no attack,
and are wholly satisfied with their present territorial circumstances, they are quite willing that the
Anglo-Saxon contract should take the Locarno form
of a guarantee of all Continental states against any
wanton aggression.

None of the Status Quo powers of the Continent,
all of whom are under challenge, will, however,
agree to any reduction in its present military
strength, while the challenge remains, and the
Anglo-Saxon powers on their part refuse such
guarantees. This is the rock upon which all dis-

armament programmes have split during the post-war years. And, of course, it is a political rock. What the situation comes down to, is that disarmament or any considerable reduction of armaments in Europe is out of the question until the great issues which divide Continental peoples, namely, the questions of the Paris Settlement, are adjusted.

The German attitude, in the matter of disarmament, is at once simple and disingenuous. The Germans were disarmed by the peace treaties. Their claim is that the terms of this disarmament involved a similar reduction in the forces of their conquerors. But since their armies cannot now be scaled down, every reduction in the armies of the Status Quo peoples proportionately reduces the force behind the peace treaties, which all the defeated peoples of the war are resolved to have revised.

Not only would reduction of the armies of the Status Quo powers thus advantage Germany, but it could, also, make war more likely, since it would diminish the odds between two groups of peoples who are hopelessly divided over the territorial issues. This is the basis of the contention of all Status Quo peoples, that reduction of armaments, in advance of political agreement, would mean not peace, but conflict. The Germans, however, with patent justice, demand equality in security, pointing out that it is inequitable that a great nation should remain measurably defenseless in the midst of an armed Europe, its military establishment legally restricted to numbers inferior to those of many relatively minor states.

In effect, however, disarmament, which in present circumstances can only mean reduction of armies, would admirably serve the German policy of treaty revision and fatally compromise that of France and her allies, who see their unity and security conditioned upon the maintenance of the territorial and military clauses of the peace treaties. And their interest in keeping the defeated states disarmed arises directly from the territorial issues.

The Italian course is perhaps even less comprehended in America than the German. Italy is frankly the most militaristic and intransigeant nation in Europe. And her present purposes and policies are directed squarely against France. But she is financially incapable of matching ships or divisions with her richer neighbor. The French system of hegemony, which is intolerable to all Italians, rests upon military supremacy. Reduction of the French army, or increase of the German, would therefore compromise the whole French system. Thus Italy, which is concentrating her attention to a striking extent upon the organization and expansion of her own military and naval forces, publicly urges treaty revision, naval holidays and

army reductions, because all would disproportion-
ately diminish French power.

Both Germany and Italy are, therefore, quite
legitimately, to be sure, taking advantage of the
concern of the Anglo-Saxon powers for disarmament to carry on their purely Nationalistic policies.
France and her allies, on the contrary, perfectly
awake to the political implications, meet the Anglo-
Saxon powers with their demand for guarantees.
The British and American people, however, ignore
the political implications of both German and Italian policies and are angered by French insistence
upon a guarantee.

But, although Anglo-Saxon criticism of France
delights and encourages the Italians and the Germans, since it serves their political ends, it accom-
plishes nothing. In fact, it makes progress even
more difficult, because it awakens both resentment
and apprehension in France. And the power of
France in the premises is absolute. She has the men,
the money and all the legal rights, which the
treaties give her. And back of her is a system of
alliances, which insures her not only military
hegemony, but diplomatic predominance alike at
Geneva, and in any continental conference. This
position, unexcelled since the great days of the
First Empire, is impregnable to attack. France cannot be coerced.

Nor, apparently in the present circumstances can she be persuaded, because all of her contentions rest upon irrefutable premises. As long as Germany and her associates of the war refuse to accept the peace treaties, French security remains under challenge and the very existence of her allies in danger. Reduction of her own military strength, together with that of her allies, unaccompanied by a political settlement or by Anglo-Saxon guarantees, would compromise her situation.

From her position, France has never budged since the Paris Conference when Clemenceau demanded and obtained a Treaty of Guarantee, later rejected by the United States Senate. The state of mind which Wilson encountered at Paris, Hughes met at Washington, Gibson at Geneva and Stimson at London. Hoover encountered the same resolution when he sought to save Germany by his moratorium proposal, without asking the view of Paris. All American "adventures in peace" have come to nothing, because all were conceived without regard to the political issues, which underly the whole European problem.

So far, however, every American Administration, from Wilson to Hoover, has steadfastly refused to acknowledge the political aspects of the problem of peace. And the reason, of course, has lain in the fact that the disaster which overtook Wilson, because he did, remains a frightening example for all of his successors. They have, therefore, uniformly attempted to limit the discussion to the problem most important for the United States, namely disarmament, as if peace were a matter which primarily had to do with ships and guns, categories and ratios.

Regularly, before each new international meeting, the American press has been crowded with endless official and semi-official statements coming from Washington, and inspired by the White House and the State Department, emphasizing the economic and ethical aspects of limitation and reduction of armaments. The size of armies, the cost of them, the burdens imposed by the last war, the horrors of modern conflict, all have been discussed endlessly and regularly, with the evident conviction that popular sentiment thus aroused in the United States, must have an irresistible momentum when it is conveyed to Europe.

Those visitors from the other side of the Atlantic who attended the Washington Conference in 1921-22, similarly voiced their utter amazement at the sudden explosion of religious emotion which attended the opening of that gathering. Prayers were sounded from the pulpits of the nation, moral agitation and public exhortation were universal. All these circumstances were frankly inexplicable to the Europeans, who came to a political conference well aware in advance that any progress must be conditioned on political bargains arrived at by barter and sale.

The delegation which represented the United States at the London Naval Conference took ship amidst the same kind of hysterical demonstration, similarly directed from Washington. But the moment that Secretary Stimson and his associates set foot upon British soil, they encountered Tardieu and Grandi, each commissioned by his nation to advocate and defend theses which were purely political. And since Stimson and Morrow were, by virtue of their implied instructions, prohibited from talking politics, the moral issues languished and the conference failed.

Washington, Geneva, London, all our disarmament conferences have failed for the same reason and in precisely the same manner. All have opened with the same American explosion of moral enthusiasm; all have ended with the same political deadlocks. Their progress could be mapped in advance like the fever chart of a known disease. The American people have passed through a preliminary stage of enormous exaltation, followed by a period of growing bewilderment and ended in a state of virtuous indignation at European peoples and their policies.

As a consequence, each international conference increases the suspicion and distrust felt on this side of the Atlantic for all European countries, and makes more difficult any form of coöperation and there can be no more ironic comment than that disclosed in the fact that international gatherings to promote peace invariably end in the accentuation of old prejudices and the stimulation of fresh misconceptions.

Nor is it possible to see an end to this situation until an American Administration is prepared to face the simple and unmistakable fact that disarmament is in Europe a political question; that progress toward limitation of armies must wait upon and keep pace with the adjustment of the great political questions, which now divide European peoples; and, finally, that no useful American contribution can be made to the adjustment of these differences, while the United States by deliberate resolution remains outside of all European political discussions.

Sound arguments can obviously be advanced for American refusal to enter the field of European politics, either to guarantee a status quo or to compel treaty revision, but it is hard to find justification for perpetual peregrinations to Europe of American missions upon evangelical tours, destitute of all authority to consider the only subjects which can possibly be discussed at any Continental meeting. And no one who has ever seen an American delegation actually at work in a European disarmament conference can fail to identify in its operations the familiar adventures of Alice in Wonderland.

In the matter of disarmament in Europe, the United States is in a position to contribute nothing. Our army and navy are not factors in European calculations. Reductions on our part, therefore, cannot promote similar reductions abroad, because we are nowhere reckoned a potential enemy and all European armaments are maintained against some specific danger. Reduction of our forces is a task for Congress not for international conference, and such reduction is the limit of our service to world disarmament. Cancellation of war debts cannot count because no nation will sacrifice security to debt payment and no European country expects to pay the war debts in any event. We are therefore, always out of the picture, despite the apparently invincible conviction on this side of the Atlantic that the mere presence of an American delegation at a League Disarmament Conference actually constitutes a contribution of formidable proportions.

Chapter Twenty-six

REPARATIONS AND WAR DEBTS

WHILE, in public discussion, revision of the territorial decisions of the Paris Treaties has occupied much attention, in practice, all efforts at revision have actually been limited to the reparations clauses. Such restriction, too, has been inevitable, because, without the consent of the nations directly concerned, no amendment of the territorial circumstances of any of the treaties is possible. And, quite naturally, no country has been prepared to consent to surrender its own territory. Nor has France been willing to agree to any modification of the military clauses of the Treaty of Versailles to permit an increase of the German army.

Even in the case of the reparations clauses of the Treaty of Versailles, progress has been hampered by the uncompromising purposes of two peoples. The Germans have been resolved not to pay reparations at all. The Americans have been determined not to cancel war debts. As a consequence of American policy, the French have insisted upon getting from the Germans what they have to pay the United States and Britain, and in addition, the costs of reconstructing their devastated area. Great Britain has similarly collected from Germany a quarter of the total payments of the Reich and from her own debtors the balance required to make up her American payments.

Reparations history since 1920 falls into three phases. In the first, the Germans undertook a campaign of indiscriminate sabotage. They resisted all treaty requirements whenever possible. They evaded the military clauses as they escaped the financial. The French replied with systematic coercion, which culminated after three years and a half in the occupation of the Ruhr. Meantime, the Anglo-Saxons, while endeavoring to restrain French coercion, made no official move to save a Germany in revolt. Germany was therefore beaten and forced to surrender. But neither during the battle, nor as a consequence of their victory, did the French collect money. On the contrary, the results of the Ruhr established the fact that although they could smash Germany at will, they could not profit by as much as a franc by the operation. The Ruhr, therefore, ended the military phase of the reparations struggle.

The second phase of the struggle opened with the intervention of the Anglo-Saxons and the effort

to translate the issue from politics to finance. The
Dawes Plan was fashioned. German finance, which
had collapsed in the great inflation crisis, was restored. The mark was stabilized by British, American and French loans. German payments were reduced and regulated, at least provisionally. Meantime, the British had endeavored summarily to end
the problem by the programme of the Balfour
Note. Reparations and war debts were both to be
abolished.

This was an admirable short cut. The remedy of
the Balfour Note once applied, all the enormous
and incalculable economic and financial disturbances of reparations would be abolished. And the
political evils would similarly be exorcised. It had
precisely one fault. It placed almost the entire cost
upon the shoulders of the American people. They
were to abandon debts, the Allies were to scrap
reparations, but the American taxpayer down at
the end of the line was to liquidate this transaction.

And the American taxpayer instantly, vocifer-
ously, passionately rejected the honor. As a consequence, the British were obliged to send Stanley
Baldwin to Washington and make a debt settlement. They were permanently out of action, so far
as the question of abolishing reparations was concerned. Henceforth they could only continue to
repeat their proposal. "Abolish reparations, cancel

debts, let America pay!" That was the British the-
sis. It was pretty cold blooded, it was essentially
selfish, but it had one merit. It could restore the
business of the world and in that business America
might eventually gain more than she could ever get
out of the attempt to collect war debts.

But there was a French aspect to this Balfour
Note. The French were seeking to collect not only
what they had to pay the Anglo-Saxons, but also
what it had cost them to repair their ruins. The
British proposal would have wiped all this latter
account out of existence, too. It would have made
France, as well as the United States, pay for the
victory. Only the Germans and the British would
get off scot-free. Also, there was the political phase.
Germany was not merely in revolt against reparations, she was asking for revision of territorial
clauses, as well as financial. And in these clauses of
the Treaty of Versailles, French security resided.
Thus on the subject of the Balfour Note the French
and Americans were on one side and the Germans
and the British on the other.

In the second phase, the politicians having grown
weary of failure, the financiers took the problem of
reparations from their limp hands. Having made
the Dawes Plan, they now translated the issue from
the realm of low politics to that of high finance
and from parliaments to the money markets. The

whole world emitted a sigh of relief. The truce of
Locarno was made. European reconstruction
seemed at last to have begun. But, in fact, what had
begun was the merry-go-round of reparations and
debts, the most preposterous episode in modern
history.

For the basic facts had not changed. The Germans were still resolved not to pay, the Americans
not to cancel. The Germans could, however, borrow, and the Americans were able and willing to
lend. Thus, beginning with 1924, a vast stream of
American money flowed into the Reich. There was
no apparent end to the flood. And the Germans,
welcoming it with both hands, employed it in two
ways. First, they paid their current reparations
charges out of it. Secondly, they sunk the remainder
in fixed improvements, in reorganizing and ration-
alizing their industry, in constructing vast swim-
ming pools, public parks, housing centres for the
masses. And they used it all up.

Meantime, the Allies, in receipt of reparations,
promptly transferred the German payments to the
United States to meet their war debts. Only the
French were able to keep a portion and, with char-
acteristic thrift, they took their payments largely in
kind, in coal, in chemicals. They put German industry to work harnessing French rivers, equipping
French harbors, developing French colonies. All

these payments in kind were accepted in forms which did not damage normal French production. German industry was now playing Santa Claus to France.

The American situation was anomalous and the British measurably the same. The American investor was buying German securities. He was lending money to Germany, Germany was paying it to the Allies, who turned it back to the American Government. Thus what was actually taking place was that the American investor was paying the Allied debts to his own government. And everybody was satisfied, because in reality no one was, as yet, paying anything, and still reparations and debts were both being paid. The Balfour Note had been rejected with indignation by the American people, but they were actually accomplishing voluntarily all that the Balfour Note undertook to bring about.

This process could have gone on indefinitely, all that was necessary was that the American investor should continue to do his part. But in 1929 he stopped. Suddenly and completely he ceased to buy German securities. But when he stopped that was the end of the financial solution of reparations as the occupation of the Ruhr had been of the political. The classic get-rich-quick operation had reached its classic ending. Germany had now to pay something outright. And she refused, alleging that it was out of the question. Finance, still unwilling to admit failure, had made the Young Plan, but that had merely nominally reduced German payments, it could not abolish them, it could not even adjust them to any proper estimate of German capacity. It had still to regulate them by American debt payments, plus French reconstruction charges.

And so the Young Plan collapsed concomitantly with the arrival of the great worldwide depression: concomitantly, not as a consequence of it, because the Germans had never seriously attempted to pay. They had never meant to pay. But, as the Young Plan collapsed, a wholly new situation was disclosed. The United States and Great Britain were now very large holders of German loans and securities. They had adventured nearly $4,000,000,-000 in the Reich. Finance had believed in its own remedies, it had convinced itself that the reparations issue had been settled.

Germany's situation was not less extraordinary. She had made the Anglo-Saxon powers partners in her business and her business was threatened with bankruptcy. She had sunk her vast borrowings in fixed improvements or her nationals had transferred them beyond her frontiers, where they were unavailable. She might be able to pay the interest on these loans, she patently could not, under existing conditions, which were in no small part of her own making, pay both reparations and interest. But reparations were a legal obligation and the French sheriff was always to be reckoned with.

It was, then, for the American and British partners in German enterprise to deal with the French sheriff, otherwise bankruptcy would come and these partners would lose much, if not all of their investments. The German's situation was perfect. He had only to wait, to warn his friends in London and New York of the facts, of what were now the facts. As for London and New York, they must play up. They could do nothing else.

The financial world was now faced with an international crisis. If Germany became bankrupt in the face of the existing depression, the disaster might go beyond calculable limits. The single way of escape was to prevent bankruptcy. And so, one day, while the masses in all countries were still oblivious to the facts of the situation, the President of the United States issued his Moratorium proposal. This opened the third and last phase of the campaign over debts and reparations and it was the stage of liquidation.

Hoover proposed that debt payments and reparation payments should come to a standstill for a year. Spared the necessity to pay $450,000,000 out of its own pocket, shored up by fresh loans, German finance might just weather the storm. It was a sim-

ple, straightforward, statesmanlike proposal. There
was nothing generous or idealistic in it. It was only
a sound business procedure applied internationally.
Like the Balfour Note, it had just one defect. It
did not give any special consideration for the $100,-
000,000 Germany was paying France in addition
to the sums France was paying her British and
American debtors. There were, to be sure, involved
intricacies, which for one year would enable France
to escape serious loss. Therefore, if France, like the
rest of the world, were primarily interested in saving Germany from bankruptcy, it was not, on the
whole, an unfair proposal.

The Germans had expected the Hoover gesture,
not exactly perhaps, but something of the sort, because at the basis of all their calculations lay the
conviction that once the Anglo-Saxons were deeply
involved in Germany's fortunes, they could not afford to let Germany sink. Now all had happened as
they had expected. Hoover had spoken, their long
battle was approaching triumphant conclusion because, they, like all other sane human beings, realized that once reparations payments were terminated, they would never begin again. No
German Government would dare undertake to re-
impose the burden—and this time a real burden—
upon the German people. All the Anglo-Saxons' interest would be engaged in avoiding a domestic

revolution in Germany, which might follow the mere attempt. Accordingly in June, 1931 the Germans waited, affording the incredible spectacle of a people on the edge of bankruptcy, and triumphant.

They had long to wait, however. What had happened amounted in effect to a deliberate undertaking on the part of the Germans to commit suicide. That was the effect of their unlimited borrowing without possibility of repayment, after they had dispersed the proceeds of these loans uneconomically. They had embarked upon financial suicide, in the firm conviction that at the fatal moment they would be restrained. They had turned on the gas, convinced that the neighbors would scent it and rush to the rescue. And the neighbors did scent it. They did rush to the rescue, but the door was locked, they could not get in. The suicide therefore started to become real. The German people began actually to suffocate.

And, of course, France was responsible. The success or failure of the Hoover Moratorium always depended upon the accuracy of the assumption that France was equally interested with everybody else, in preventing the German bankruptcy. But that was not the case. On the contrary, the French were primarily interested in preserving the whole structure of the Treaty of Versailles against a German attack which was designed to destroy it in every detail. They saw what Germany had done. They recognized that it was in effect suicide. But they were also convinced that Germany had never meant to die, that she had counted upon the rescue, which the Hoover Moratorium had undertaken. In the crisis they were calm, unbelievably cool behind the excited outbursts of their press. They were willing that Germany should be saved, but not at their expense, not at the sacrifice of their political or financial rights, but the political always came first.

So France met the Hoover Moratorium, not by a surrender, but by a prolonged negotiation, which disclosed the fact that Anglo-Saxon coercion was not going to bring French submission. Bruening's excursion to Paris and London confirmed the impression. Paris stood firm. And, as a consequence, the suicide was real, after all. Germany did become bankrupt. And the costs of her bankruptcy, ironically enough, had to be borne by her friends, not by her enemies. Germany had made the British and American investors partners in her national establishment up to the limit of their willingness to buy German securities, but instead of saving her from the consequences of her actions, they now shared in the effects of her disaster.

And, at that, Germany might have won. In fact she came as near to winning as in the World War itself. Again she made just one fatal miscalculation. She was so sure of the Anglo-Saxon power to control France that she totally disregarded the French, just as she had dismissed the Americans, when she embarked upon her submarine campaign during the World War. And, dismissing the French as negligible, she had recourse to the Anschluss manœuvre, to satisfy the growing tumult of the National Socialists at home.

But for that the French might have yielded. They might have been stampeded by the Hoover Moratorium or persuaded at the London Conference. They had the law on their side but their isolation was far from comfortable. By one swift, devastating manœuvre, however, the statesmen of the Reich had revived in France the mood of Verdun. At the decisive moment the French people were united in the spirit of "They shall not pass." The Austro-German proposal had touched French safety, it had challenged the whole French system of security and influence in Europe. As a consequence, at Paris and London, while the Americans and Britons talked finance and peace, the French thought simply of politics.

Nevertheless, as a result of the Hoover Moratorium all of the war debts and at least the greater part of reparations are dead, as dead as Queen Anne. The Moratorium must be extended automatically, not for one year, but indefinitely. No German government will ever be able to impose all or any large part of the old burdens again. The British and American investors will hardly care to risk the National-Socialist, or Communist explosion that would result. France may temporarily save the unconditional part of the Young Plan payments, the part, which is sacred beyond the touch of an ordinary moratorium. But the Hoover Moratorium has already touched even this. The American Congress may stand firm against debt cancellation. It can stand forever, now. For the Hoover Moratorium established the relation of debts and reparations inescapably—beyond even political hocus-pocus.

Hoover did not save Germany from bankruptcy or the world from the consequences of that disaster. That was always beyond his power after the German adventure in Anschluss. He miscalculated the situation, he ignored the political aspect. He could not believe the French would dare to resist the wave of world opinion which would be stirred by his gesture. He did not take into account the counterwave of public opinion his move would start in France, where it was interpreted as a purely pro-German and even Anti-French operation. He did not understand the politics of the situation, he was thinking only of the economics and the finance. So were the American people; therefore, like the

President, they were at first puzzled and then angered.

Both started with the assumption that the salvation of Germany was a necessity for the financial stability of the world. And that was perhaps true. It was also the basic calculation of the German people in their battle with France over the whole question of the Treaty of Versailles. But the French people, having to choose between the world disaster incident to German bankruptcy, and their own disaster which must follow the effective breaching of the contract of Versailles, saw the former eventuality less formidable for themselves. They may have been right or wrong, both on the moral and on the material side, but, in any event, they were successful. Germany fell, but the Treaty of Versailles lives. It is still the law of Europe, and as a result of their realistic policy in the summer and autumn of 1931, French power and prestige have profited immeasurably.

Nevertheless, Herbert Hoover cancelled war debts and reduced reparations to the narrow limits of the unconditional payments of the Dawes Plan. These, France has still the power and the right to collect, and the sums involved are relatively so small that for a time Germany may find it more profitable to meet French terms than to court a new disaster, particularly if she can borrow the money from France. Yet even these payments will not endure long and for a simple reason, the reason which explains the failure of both the politicians and the financiers, and the fallacy underlying the attempt to collect any international obligations growing out of the World War.

In point of fact, despite all the years of controversy, it has never been proven that Germany could not pay large sums abroad on account of reparations. It has never been established that the debts settlements made by the United States with her wartime allies, settlements essentially and inherently generous regarded solely from the material aspect, exceeded the capacity of these nations to pay. What has been made clear beyond all challenge is something quite different, which both the financiers and the politicians ignored.

The collection of reparations and of war debts is equally impossible for the obvious reason that under modern democratic conditions no government which depends upon the people for its existence, which must shortly seek re-election by popular vote, can afford to undertake to impose upon its peoples war-debt burdens which involve a lowering of the standard of national life, the denial to youth of the opportunities all parents demand for their children, the limitation upon national independence which such foreign payments insure.

No democratic government can live, which assumes in the eyes of its own people the guise of a mere collecting agency for foreign creditors. This is equally true, whether the creditor has been an ally or an enemy in war. In the latter case, however, resentment is intensified and passion further excited. The decline of the prestige of the republic within the Reich has been almost uniquely due to the fact that it has been condemned to stand before the German people asking them to assume burdens which in the eyes of these people must inevitably appear tribute. For, in effect, in all but legal form, they are tribute.

Such payments are possible, in a case like that after the Franco-Prussian War, when Bismarck exacted no more than a billion from the French. For the payment was almost immediate and the tangible compensation was the unconditional release of France from all German restraint, military, political or financial. But the reparations and war debts were burdens for three generations. Age, Youth, and Posterity were alike to be harnessed to the task of paying for a war, for which Age alone had any responsibility.

The thing was not only contrary to reason, but to nature itself. And, in fact, the whole attempt broke down just as soon as the victors had seized all the tangible assets they could lay their hands upon. Thereafter the American people began to pay their government the Allied debts by lending Germany money. But even this device did not abolish the German rebellion, because the German people, while not actually paying money, went through the motions and saw the mortgage upon their future in the shape of foreign holdings of German securities expanding to astronomical proportions, while their own fortunes visibly worsened. Inescapably they became victims of a delusion of persecution and experienced the emotions of an enslaved people. And, while they were still under the menace of having to pay the war debts, the Allied peoples themselves disclosed precisely the same state of mind.

The Hoover Moratorium put a stop to something, which cannot be set in motion again, the twin Humpty-Dumpties of reparations and war debts have tumbled definitively. What remains to be disclosed is how long it will take the American people—and perhaps the French as well—to reconcile themselves to the accomplished fact. What the American people have eventually to recognize is that the value of a debt depends ultimately either upon the power of the creditor to collect or upon the degree to which the debtor regards his honor or his interest as engaged. In the case of war debts and reparations there is no power to collect. The French proved that when they occupied the Ruhr. Nor is there any means of making the masses of any country feel that their honor or interest is engaged in voluntarily meeting obligations which have their origin in war.

Since the American people refused to recognize this fundamental fact and continued to accept the jargon of politicians about the sacredness of contracts and the clap-trap of financiers about the capacity to pay, Europe fell back upon the endless chain device, by which we lent money to Germany and Germany handed it over to our war debtors, who transferred it back to us. This system can be started again, if we or the French are prepared to make fresh loans to Germany, but not otherwise. What remains to be discovered is whether we shall be able to collect the private loans. But war debts belong with Fenian bonds.

For the rest, the Hoover Moratorium and the Locarno Pacts which, at the least, put an end to that other and equal folly of treating the Germans as an outcast and guilty people, represent the positive achievements of the post-war era. And the former also represents the maximum of treaty revision which has ever been possible since the Paris Conference. Congress and the politicians have still to overtake events and the spectacle will be pleasing, but the result is assured. Meantime, since, not for financial, not even for political, but solely for human reasons, peace was never possible while war debts and reparations endured, and since both are now gone, the world is at least that much nearer to peace.

Chapter Twenty-seven

WHY THEY FAILED

ALL the experiments in peace of the post-war years have, then, failed. And in every case the explanation is the same. They have failed because they were based upon the assumption that what existed was peace and that the task was to preserve it. But, actually, peace did not exist. The nations which had confronted each other during the long years of the great conflict still remained in presence. There were changes in the firing-lines. The Anglo-Saxons had gone home. New combatants had arrived and old had been removed as casualties, but the battle continued.

The issue, too, was unmistakable. The vanquished refused to accept the terms which the victors had imposed upon them in the Paris Settlement. As for the conquerors, they were resolved not to sacrifice the fruits of their triumph. Thus the struggle which had been interrupted by the Armistice of Rethondes was resumed after the ratification of the Treaty of Versailles.

Since the defeated were now disarmed, they could not again employ weapons. They had no artillery, tanks or gas, they had neither machine guns nor airplanes. As a consequence, the victors were, in their turn, unable to employ armies or guns in action, although their supply was unlimited. They were obliged to fall back upon treaty rights, upon sanctions authorized by treaty-law, and upon economic and financial reprisals.

But it was war, nevertheless. And the supreme illusion of the post-war world lies precisely in the assumption that armed conflict alone is war. In reality, war is the pursuit of policy by all possible means. In the years after the Paris Settlement, arms were unavailable, but by every other means peoples pursued national policies, and these policies were identical with those which nations had hitherto supported by arms.

What happened at the close of the World War was at once fantastic, and is now unmistakable. All peoples solemnly, sincerely, passionately renounced war. Its agonies, miseries, horrors were before all eyes, and every race and people once and for all resolved never to go through it again. But, in reality, what peoples renounced was not war. They did not discard irreconcilable national policies. They did not drop rival racial aspirations. They simply declared that henceforth they would not use arms to establish these purposes. But they were still resolved to employ all other means—and did. They used tariff, finance, trade, commerce, even the experiments in peace, to make war.

What resulted was war, because in the minds of the German people, who revolted against the Treaty of Versailles, in the minds of the Magyars, who similarly resisted the Treaty of Trianon, all that counted in life, all that men and women held dear, national independence, national and racial unity, everything was for them at stake and would be lost, if the treaties stood unmodified. But for the nations who had gained by the treaties, precisely the same things were involved. It was life or death for all, as all saw the issues.

When, therefore, the Anglo-Saxon peoples began to offer their several prescriptions of peace, designed to keep order in a peaceful world, the quarrelling peoples of the Continent instantly seized upon these pacific programmes for controversial purposes. Briand and the statesmen of the Little Entente stormed the League of Nations and made it the headquarters of Status Quo. The Germans, after Stresemann's death, tried to dislodge the enemy and to shape the League to their purpose of treaty revision. Henceforth Geneva was a battlefield, not the capital of world tranquillity.

America brought forward the Kellogg Pact.

France welcomed it, Briand adopted it. But shortly there came a suggestion to provide it with teeth. To bite whom? Anyone who attempted to achieve by arms what all the nations in revolt against the peace treaties were endeavoring to accomplish by all other means. A consultative pact was proposed. To consult about what? About common action against any people who set out to accomplish by force what the Germans, Austrians, Magyars and Bulgars were already striving to accomplish although disarmed.

Britain and America pressed for disarmament. The Germans themselves, forcibly disarmed by the peace treaties, seized upon this project as a means of disarming their enemies. If they could only get enough guns out of French hands they would acquire not merely equality in security, but equality in any future battle. But the French responded by a demand for Anglo-Saxon guarantees. Guarantees against what? Against the dangers they maintained armies to meet. And, such guarantees being refused, deadlock resulted.

Last of all, treaty revision was suggested, this time by Anglo-Saxon Liberals like Borah, eager to promote peace in Europe. But this was precisely what the Germans were fighting for, it was the issue of battle. And, encouraged by this foreign gesture, the Germans and Austrians promptly attempted revision by tariff union. But in vain, for France responded. She did not move a soldier, the canvas did not come off a single "seventy-five," but Germany and Austria were compelled to surrender. Money accomplished on the stock exchanges of the world what arms had achieved at the Marne.

Meantime, finance and business had been working on parallel lines. They, too, had accepted the transparent inveracity. American and British bankers and industrialists, alike, had assumed that the European Continent was at peace. They undertook to organize this peace upon a business and financial basis. The Dawes Plan was their first venture. And, because the Ruhr War was over and both contestants exhausted, the bankers were allowed a hearing. The politicians cooperated, and Locarno emerged. But in reality, it was only an armistice, a truce of exhaustion, for the wills of peoples remained unshaken.

As a consequence, Locarno faded. Thoiry turned out to have been only a luncheon, and nothing more. The financiers tried the Young Plan, but that collapsed briefly. For the war was on again, this time in grand style. It had, indeed, become faster and more furious than before. Stahlhelm hosts thundered a new menace at France from Coblenz, and from Breslau at Poland. Polish Nationalism took up the challenge and German newspapers were soon crowded with tales of Polish "atrocities." Already this incredible peace had come to atrocities!

But Washington and London, Wall Street and "the City" refused to face the fact. MacDonald and Hoover sat beside the waters of the Rapidan and discussed naval disarmament. American and British loans flowed into Central Europe, for the League of Nations had now "saved" both Vienna and Budapest. The London Naval Conference failed, the Preliminary Disarmament Conference accomplished nothing, Briand's Pan-European plan was still-born; all economic prescriptions broke down. The German Election of September, 1930, came to defy the most robust of optimists. The Austro-German Tariff Union exploded like the shots of Serajevo. Meantime, Washington and London still continued to prepare for a disarmament conference.

France, however, was preparing for something else, she was preparing for the next campaign. She had begun to get ready when the Bruening Cabinet had snatched the battle-cry of territorial revision from the Hitler mobs. And so the great crisis of June, 1931, arrived. British and American publics suddenly perceived the whole financial and economic edifice of Central Europe toppling. But it was always bound to topple in the end if the war continued long enough.

War, by all other means save arms may not work

its havoc as rapidly as war with great guns and intensive bombardments, but in modern industrial life, under the existing economic system, peoples cannot indefinitely fight each other by tariffs, embargoes, financial coercion, by everything except guns, and not, in the end, break glass. Yet British and American finance continued to conduct business as usual on the slopes of the volcano.

As a consequence, when the inevitable at last happened, British and American captains of finance and industry found themselves suddenly in exactly the predicament of British "trippers" and American tourists, when, without warning in the calm days of July, 1914, the heavens opened and a torrent of mobilization orders descended. Even then, London and Washington would not believe the evidence of their senses. They saw what must happen unless something were done—but they still believed something could be done.

So Hoover launched his Moratorium. Another president had acted similarly, in 1916, while America was still neutral, and saw, with that objectivity permitted to neutrals alone, that the World War, which had already been proceeding for three years, must, if it continued, work irremediable injury to all mankind. And Paris and London desired peace; Berlin and Vienna were eager to see the end of the long agony. But when Woodrow Wilson supplemented his gesture by adding the words "Peace without victory," the Allies and the Central Powers both looked askance. It was peace *with* victory that they were all fighting for.

It was that way again in the long days of July, 1931, when so many anniversaries of 1914 passed not quite unnoticed. For twelve years, save in the periods of truce due to exhaustion, the German people had conducted an attack upon the whole system of European law and order, which had been based upon their defeat, and in their eyes doomed them to the condition of a subject nation, and a tribute-paying race. During all these same years, the French people had resisted that attack, which was for them a threat to their existence. A lost battle now, as always, meant the collapse of all their system of order and security; it could be the preface to fresh invasion.

One people had to surrender. It was the single conceivable escape from destruction as complete as that of authentic war. Hoover's gesture was made at the last possible moment. But neither people did, or could surrender, because for each, the battle was for absolutes. The Anglo-Saxons talked about money, business, morals, all in vain. Germany would not give in and France would not yield. Thus, in the end, the peaceful war, the war without battle, produced precisely the same economic and financial results that all wars must bring, all shocks between peoples who have dismissed from their calculations every other consideration save that of victory.

German bankruptcy arrived. The disaster spread to Central Europe. Britain was shaken by the convulsion. The lives of millions of peoples were affected. The extent of the disaster could not be measured, and may not be ascertained in our generation. But the war did not end, because the will to war existed in the minds and hearts and brains of the peoples in combat. The economic and financial life of a whole continent, its social foundations had been shaken and continued to rock, but victorious France and defeated Germany still confronted each other in Geneva, in Paris, in London as they had faced each other at every moment since Brockdorff-Rantzau, in the Hall of Mirrors, had remained seated while Clemenceau pronounced the sentence of Versailles.

In this fashion, Herbert Hoover's experiment failed in its turn as all experiments moral, political and financial have failed in the post-war era, because all have been designed to preserve a peace which did not exist. None of them provided the slightest means for ending a war in full progress. And that problem still remains intact.

Part Five

CONCLUSION

Chapter Twenty-eight

BACK TO LOCARNO

CAN Europe keep the peace? This question which
the whole English-speaking world has been asking
with increasing anxiety for a dozen years, at once
betrays its origin and evades the issue. For the real
question is whether Europe will accept the only
peace now available. The problem is all there. The
situation is equally clear. The territorial issues
which divide European peoples are insoluble. At
least, they are insoluble in the present temper of
peoples and in accord with their present conception
of their rights. National policies are irreconcilable
for the same reason. The experiments in peace have
failed because they were designed to guarantee existing order against future anarchy. But the anarchy
was already there.

Europe then faces a simple alternative. It must
accept some provisional system of order, or the
complete disintegration of what contemporary
mankind counts civilization is inevitable. Seventeen
years of almost continuous conflict, interrupted only

by incomplete truce, have reduced the whole Continent to a state of economic and social disorder unparalleled since the Thirty Years War. The ordinary processes of international relations in an orderly world have broken down. Nations are bankrupt, trade is reduced to barter, money has lost its value, even the pound sterling has faltered. The unemployed millions are meagrely fed by public treasuries, themselves inadequately filled by taxation which is extortionate. The miseries of the so-called peace of today, miseries reaching to every human being within national limits, defy exaggeration. It is clear that what has been going on since July, 1914, cannot continue.

What, then, is the practical alternative? How has the present situation come to pass? Quite simply, the peoples who were defeated in the World War, the Germans, the Austrians, the Hungarians, refused to accept the terms which were imposed upon them after surrender. They resumed the conflict. It was their right. Those terms represented in their eyes the destruction of all that they held dear and sacred. They constituted the utter denial of their hopes for the present and their dreams for the future. Americans would have done the same.

But what has been the result of this war after war? Germany is today bankrupt and beaten. Austria and Hungary have come to the edge of ruin and have surrendered again. They have given up the fight and sought and obtained such terms as they could get from their conquerors. Only Germany is left and she is patently helpless. She has a single choice. She can follow the example of her allies of the war and abandon the fight, or she can throw herself into the arms of the Nationalist elements within her own boundaries and try to continue the struggle.

The German situation is, however, worse today than ever before for the simple reason that, as a consequence of the last convulsion, Germany has exhausted the possibilities of aid from without. The Anglo-Saxon peoples, in all the post-war years, have increasingly sympathized with the Germans. They have seen justice in many of their claims. And, particularly in the reparations circumstances of the Treaty of Versailles, they have discovered wrongs, which they have endeavored to mitigate. But they can do no more. While the fundamental causes of the British financial crisis of September, 1931, were many and various, the precipitating occasion was the German crash.

Britain and the United States have lent billions to the Germans in the belief that economic recovery would bring about political appeasement. But they can and will lend no more. The British problem henceforth must be to recover the loans temporarily "frozen" in the Reich. American policy can hardly be different, and for both countries the only hope of recovering these loans must be through the restoration of peace and order.

Unless the Germans are actually resolved upon national suicide, unless they are unalterably determined to follow the example of Samson, so familiar in their present conversation, they must end a battle they have now no hope of winning. They must give up the agitation at home and abroad for the revision of the territorial decisions of the Treaty of Versailles. The Polish Corridor is lost for them as Alsace-Lorraine was lost for France after Sedan, to remain lost for almost half a century. Like the Reichsland, the Polish Corridor can only be regained by war and, like France in 1870, Germany cannot today make war to recover it. Sooner or later, therefore, she will have to follow the example of France.

For twelve years the German people have clung to the illusion that their resistance to the Treaty of Versailles would, in the end, insure revision of the territorial as well as the reparations clauses. They have counted upon Anglo-Saxon aid to achieve this end. They have been certain that Soviet Russia would overwhelm Poland, as it narrowly missed doing in 1920. They have expected Poland to collapse from internal chaos. None of these things has happened or can, now, in any useful time.

The Germans must, therefore, for all present time, renounce a hope beyond realization. In point of fact, the hope will remain. The purpose to recover the lost provinces of the East will survive as immutable as the similar hope of the French after the Treaty of Frankfort. But, like France, Germany will, in the end, have to live within frontiers which she holds unjust and will continue to regard as intolerable.

Even if they have for the present lost their battle for territorial revision, however, the Germans have nevertheless won much by their resistance. All but the unconditional payments of the Young Plan are done for. Two-thirds of the annual tribute has been abolished and the rest will not in any event long endure. When she began her struggle, Germany was liable under the Treaty of Versailles for a sum in excess of $1,500,000,000 annually. At most, the unconditional payments of the Young Plan will not much exceed $150,000,000.

Germany has won other things, too. The Pacts of Locarno ended her isolation. Henceforth, she appeared at Geneva as a great power with not a little of her prestige of the pre-war era, at least during the lifetime of Stresemann. The visit of Laval to Hindenburg destroyed the stupid pretense of "war criminals." The legend of the "guilty nation" has long expired. Morally as well as materially, Germany has won her battle against the decisions of the Paris Settlement.

Today, however, Germany faces a France which was victorious in the World War, has triumphed in the post-war struggles and on the military, financial and diplomatic sides now occupies an impregnable position beyond the reach of Anglo-Saxon persuasion and coercion alike. The price of French aid, without which Germany cannot get on, is a truce to agitation for territorial revision. The price is high, the cost to Germanism in the east will be unmistakable. But escape is nowhere else discoverable. No one could expect the German people to make any formal renunciation, such as they actually made in the case of Alsace-Lorraine, in the Locarno pacts. To require it would be stupid and futile.

In the Locarno Pacts, however, Germany did renounce the right to recover the Corridor by violence and that renunciation still stands. Never abrogated, it has simply been ignored. No new humiliation is then involved in asking the German people to live in accordance with an agreement already accepted by them, which today continues to be the law of Europe. Thanks to that agreement, too, Germany obtained five years of relative calm, the evacuation of the Rhineland years in advance of the treaty date, the abolition of all military and financial supervision within the Reich. Had Stresemann lived, further reduction in financial payments might have been made by agreement but events have brought that about now.

Financially and economically, German prosperity has not been materially affected by the loss of the Corridor. In itself, it is a relatively poor region of heaths and forests and sand. Strategically and politically, it is even more valuable than Alsace-Lorraine, while sentimentally and symbolically, it has the same value. Upper Silesia, by contrast, is an economic loss as considerable as that of the Reichsland to France. But the alternative to submitting to loss now is a new war without hope of victory.

If Germany consents to a renewal of Locarno, even if formal action does not go beyond the suppression of domestic tumult, and foreign agitation then the association between French, British and German statesmen at Geneva, so profitable for all of Europe in the Stresemann era, would not only be possible but inevitable. The League would, in its turn, profit immeasurably: its machinery is available, but it is worthless as long as the Swiss city remains a battleground of French and German policies.

Franco-German reconciliation, by contrast, can be neither a simple nor a rapid process. What is possible is for the two people to do business profitably together if they can even tacitly agree upon a political truce. They did that after 1870 and German need for Lorraine iron and French for Ruhr coal and chemicals supply a natural basis for exchange. Germany will not forget her territorial losses nor France cease to be concerned over security in this generation. But the immediate problem is one not of future friendship but of present fighting. Locarno was the only practical expedient that has been evolved since the war, a solution not of the basic issues but only of the immediate problem of avoiding anarchy and establishing some system of European order, however provisional and incomplete. In a new Thoiry, such as was sketched by Laval and Briand in their conferences with Bruening and Curtius in Berlin in September, 1931, not only British but also Americans could cooperate usefully.

One further fact is unmistakable. If the Germans, in the face of the existing conditions, continue their policy of resistance, they will presently find themselves in the same situation as at the close of the World War. Without regard to the moral aspects of the issues involved, such a policy will promptly appear in the eyes of British and American publics seeking order and reconstruction the sole barrier to both. Thus a Germany dominated by a National-

Socialist dictatorship would find itself again in the situation of the Reich at the moment the Treaty of Versailles was made and the consequences to the German people of a new isolation might be as unfortunate as those of the old.

There remains the question of Central Europe. It will be improved by a return to Locarno by France and Germany, but not materially, not enough. In the end, there is no solution of the problem of the Danubian area, save through the reconstruction of the economic associations which formerly united the present territories of Austria, Czecho-Slovakia and Hungary. Political reunion is out of the question now and perhaps ever, but, to live, these peoples must trade together. And, despite all that has been written and argued about the Anschluss, it has never been demonstrated that it would bring any material relief to the Austrians. All their markets, business, traditions economically are with the peoples of their old empire.

If the Czechs, who must under French inspiration do the work, cannot find a basis for immediate economic association with both Austria and Hungary and also for eventual frontier readjustment with the Magyars, they are themselves doomed. They will one day be partitioned between the Germans and the Hungarians and disappear once more as after the Battle of the White Mountain. But even an economic association with Hungary must inevitably restore the relations between Slovakia and Budapest. Economically, Czecho-Slovakia, Hungary and Austria cannot exist independently and a restoration of trade relations would almost incalculably modify racial animosities.

France would favor, Italy would oppose such a programme, which in Italian eyes would envisage at least a partial restoration of a state, long the hereditary enemy of the Savoy Monarchy. Yet, it is far from impossible that Fascist statesmanship will presently perceive that this offers the single avenue of escape from the immediate menace of the Anschluss and also the promise of an eventual disintegration of the Little Entente, now a pillar of French hegemony. For, once the dangers, against which the French alliance insures Czecho-Slovakia, disappear, all the material interests of this state are comprehended in Central Europe itself.

A return to Locarno by France, Germany and Great Britain; acceptance of the contemporary inviolability of the status quo in respect of the Polish Corridor and Upper Silesia; a new policy of economic cooperation in the Danubian region, backed by financial assistance from the outside; these steps, combined with the restoration of the moral prestige of the League of Nations, which would follow and the removal of the débris of reparations and war debts, which must accompany them, are the present limits of practical statesmanship in Europe. Restricted as they patently are, however, they would meet the single necessity, which is for immediate political truce and prompt financial and economic reconstruction.

All the vast, complicated and inevitably controversial programme for the establishment of a permanent system of peace in Europe, is manifestly the task of a tranquil Continent. Reorganization of the League of Nations, amendment of the Kellogg Pact, disarmament and territorial revision must, in the very nature of things, be the issues of battle in a Europe at war. What is required today is not an ideal solution of the problems of international life in Europe but a chance for Europe to live. The experiments in peace will go on, for the organization of peace is a continuous process, but the world can no longer wait for solutions.

The major cause of the universal misunderstanding of the problem of peace in the post-war world has arisen from the belief that, as a result of the great convulsion, mankind was going to find some new, complete, all-sufficing moral solution for its political difficulties. From the enormous and unmeasured agony of the general catastrophe, all peoples looked up suddenly hoping to see in the heavens a new revelation. They welcomed Woodrow Wilson as a Messiah, because they were conscious of the need of a new faith. They believed in the possibility of a miracle, because they had reached the point where only a miracle seemed of the least avail.

But no miracle arrived. The war came and went. The peace settlements were made and still all of the old, familiar elements in the European problem remained. The issues growing out of racial and economic details still endured. They were facts. But for twelve years European peoples, encouraged by Anglo-Saxon ignorance and idealism, crass selfishness and sound common sense have been trying to abolish these facts or to stabilize forever the outward form, which they received at the hands of the makers of the peace treaties. All mankind has desired peace, but each people has had its own prescription and, in the aggregate, these prescriptions have been irreconcilable.

In the end, European peoples and nations have well-nigh committed suicide without modifying the facts. Now, at the very edge of ultimate ruin, Europe—and perhaps the world as well—has reached a point where it must adjust its existence to inescapable truths or destroy itself by continuing cease-

lessly but uselessly to fight against them. The era of
idealistic solutions is over; the period of realistic
adjustments must, inevitably, be at hand. And Locarno was—and remains—a policy of constructive
realism.

Chapter Twenty-nine

THE CRISIS IN DEMOCRACY

THERE is, however, one other aspect to the general world problem. What exists today is primarily a crisis in Democracy itself. In Anglo-Saxon countries, Democracy has been accepted as a doctrine of order, because it evolved slowly and steadily amongst peoples who had already achieved ethnic and territorial unity without regard to other races or nations. Each, too, while Democracy was in full development, was engaged in a process of imperial expansion. Only once in American history—and that in the case of the Civil War—did democratic doctrine threaten to destroy that unity upon which national prosperity and security were based. And, with ruthless realism, the American Democracy sacrificed its principles to practical considerations and put down the Rebellion.

By contrast, on the European Continent, Democracy has always been a religion of revolution. Ever since the French Revolution, it has been engaged in the destruction of the existing order of authority.

It has been uninterruptedly at work vindicating the
rights of man against domestic government and the
rights of races against coalesced governments. The
whole history of the Nineteenth Century is the history of the democratic assault upon the system set
up by the Congress of Vienna, which was the nega-
tion of Democracy. The World War, itself, was
the final convulsion of the struggle which began in
1792.

But when, in 1918, Monarchy everywhere collapsed and Democracy, by virtue of its victory, acquired full and complete authority, although it had
bestowed liberty upon all peoples, it was unable to
provide any system of authority to preserve order
between them. The reason was obvious. It had been
engaged solely in destruction. It had made war
upon the Holy Alliance, the Concert of Europe, the
Central Powers, which still in 1914 in all of the
middle of Europe, sustained an old order against
democratic principles. But in 1918 Democracy was
in fact the victim of the very completeness of its
own triumph.

The breakdown of order in post-war Europe, or,
more exactly, the failure to re-establish order, arose
from the fact that Democracy had been the doctrine
of the absolute rights of peoples and the problem
of peace, after the World War, was to subordinate
the rights of individual nations and races to the

collective right of all mankind to order. That Democracy could not do, because all peoples and races
were able to invoke democratic principles against
any such assertion of authority. The League of Nations, which was an instinctive attempt on the part
of Democracy to escape from the *impasse* in which
it found itself, failed because, while most nations
joined, all refused to abridge their own absolute
rights. They denied the League authority, and without authority it could do nothing.

But the graver aspect of the situation resulted
from the fact that Democracy was, in itself, an
Eighteenth Century conception of individual rights,
which were now become totally incompatible with
the physical facts of an industrial civilization.
Science, machinery, invention, had transformed the
world which had existed at the moment of the
French Revolution. The liberty which Democracy
had set out to vindicate was now irreconcilable
with that unity which was the prerequisite of the
modern world.

As a consequence, the attempt to reorganize the
European Continent on the basis of race and in
accordance with the principle of self-determination,
produced utter and unimaginable ruin. It was like
dissolving a great modern railway system into its
original elements and permitting the operators of
the separated sections to run these lines solely with

regard to local traffic and parochial interests. That
was what happened after the peace treaties were
made. That is what is still going on.

Within nations, peoples soon perceived the need
of order. Thus they had recourse not merely to the
super-nationalist dictatorships of Mussolini and
Pilsudski, but to a decree-law régime in Germany,
to a National Cabinet in Britain without precedent
in peace-time. France turned all its financial fortunes over to Poincaré. Everywhere parliaments
were on the decline. Political parties based upon
old-time principles had proven equally helpless.
Liberalism was dead everywhere, because the battle
for liberty had been won.

Actually the situation of Democracy after 1918
was singularly like that of Monarchy after 1815. It
had been established at Paris as Divine Right and
had been re-enthroned at Vienna. But it was now
under direct challenge. The Russian Revolution
occupied in respect of Democracy the position Democracy had filled in the face of Monarchy after
Waterloo. For the first time, it was on the defensive.
For a hundred years, it had been abolishing authority and now it was authority, there was none other.

Conscious of this Communist threat, it instinctively followed the example of Monarchy, it fell
into the throes of reaction. And the reaction was
nationalistic. After 1815, Monarchy, under chal-

lenge, undertook by going to the utmost limits of royalistic excess to abolish the surviving spirit of the French Revolution. The reaction of Democracy was precisely the same attempt to abolish a patent danger by a resort to more intense nationalism. Internationalism as illustrated by Moscow was the peril; the remedy was, therefore, nationalism, incredible, unlimited, ferocious.

But inevitably this reaction produced still greater economic ruin. For nationalism itself was the disease from which mankind was suffering. It multiplied the barriers and obstacles to the flow of international trade and commerce, which were the life blood of a modern industrial system. And, in due course, that reaction brought us to the point at which we have now arrived. Curiously enough, too, Democracy did not merely attack Communism, it also assailed Finance and for the same reason. For Communism and Capitalism are essentially international in their conceptions. And Democracy, since it was national, since its whole doctrine was that of the rights of individual peoples, instinctively felt the menace to itself inherent in both.

Such is the larger crisis of Democracy and its bearing upon the more immediate problem of peace in Europe is patent. The only possible form of peace now discoverable upon this planet must be international. Either Democracy will discover a technique for regulating the liberties which it has bestowed and adjusting the rights which it has established, or it will make way in its turn for a new political gospel of another age.

Meantime, there are at least signs that what has happened within European states is beginning to occur in international relations. Peoples appear on the point of recognizing that the present problem is a problem of peace and not of rights, of collective order and not of individual liberty. The great crisis of 1931 following upon the World depression seems already to have had an effect. Nationalism, despite all its outward show, is confronted now with the unmistakable alternative of plunging peoples to ultimate ruin or of yielding to the inescapable logic of events.

Can Europe keep the peace? Can it accept that peace which has already been made, which during the twelve years since the Paris Conference has submitted to very far-reaching revision by attrition, if not by agreement? Unquestionably, for the alternative is collective suicide. What is not clear is whether Europe can actually make enduring peace under Democracy. Obviously it can no longer continue the effort to reconcile a Twentieth Century industrial world with an Eighteenth Century doctrine. The task is not to adjust life to a dogma but a dogma to life; not to make the world safe for Democracy but Democracy safe for the world.

That is the ultimate problem of peace in Europe. And, whatever solution may be found, it will not be long in communicating itself to this side of the Atlantic. For isolation is not merely one, but perhaps also the last, of the illusions of Democracy.

Index